Activities

for ADULTS
with LEARNING
DISABILITIES

of related interest

The Accessible Games Book
Katie Marl
ISBN 978 1 85302 830 4

Working with People with Learning Disabilities
Theory and Practice
David Thomas and Honor Woods
ISBN 978 1 85302 973 8

Day Services for People with Learning Disabilities
Edited by Philip Seed
ISBN 978 1 85302 339 2
Case Studies for Practice

Guide to Mental Health for Families and Carers of People with
Intellectual Disabilities
Edited by Geraldine Holt, Anastasia Gratsa, Nick Bouras, Theresa Joyce, Mary Jane Spiller and Steve Hardy
ISBN 978 1 84310 277 9

Learning Disability in Focus
The Use of Photography in the Care of People with a
Learning Disability
Eve and Neil Jackson
ISBN 978 1 85302 693 5

Person-Centred Planning and Care Management with People
with Learning Disabilities
Edited by Paul Cambridge and Steven Carnaby
ISBN 978 1 84310 131 4

Activities

for **ADULTS** with **LEARNING** **DISABILITIES**

Having Fun, Meeting Needs

HELEN SONNET AND ANN TAYLOR

Jessica Kingsley Publishers
London and Philadelphia

First published in 2009
by Jessica Kingsley Publishers
116 Pentonville Road
London N1 9JB, UK
and
400 Market Street, Suite 400
Philadelphia, PA 19106, USA

www.jkp.com

Library of Congress Cataloging in Publication Data

Sonnet, Helen.
  Activities for adults with learning disabilities / Helen Sonnet and Ann Taylor.
    p. cm.
  ISBN 978-1-84310-975-4 (alk. paper)
  1. Learning disabled. 2. Occupational therapy. 3. Adult day care centers--Activity
    programs. 4. Nursing homes--Recreational activities. I. Taylor, Ann. II. Title.
  LC4818.S66 2009
  371.9'0475--dc22

                                                        2009005092

British Library Cataloguing in Publication Data
A CIP catalogue record for this book is available from the British Library

ISBN 978 1 843 10975 4

Printed and bound in Great Britain by
Athenaeum Press, Gateshead, Tyne and Wear

Note: It is not the intention of the authors to endorse any particular brand over another.

CONTENTS

NOTE FROM THE AUTHORS

When my daughter started to attend our local Gateway Club, which organized activities for and with people with learning disabilities, I agreed to remain with her for the first few times and keep her company, as she didn't know any of the other members. It seemed only natural to pitch in and assist whilst I was there and, learning that help was always in short supply, I have remained in that role ever since.

As an experienced teacher and writer of activity books for children, I was immediately impressed by the quality of the organized events. The leader, Ann Taylor, had many brilliant, creative ideas and all the members participated and seemed to enjoy the sessions that she organized. The activities were interesting and varied and also helped to evolve useful social and life skills.

I discovered that Ann had developed her programme over the years, without access to helpful literature and a further investigation proved that there was a dearth of books of activities for adults with learning difficulties. I thought that it would be a good idea to combine our talents and expertise to share these valuable session ideas with other people working in similar clubs or residential homes.

We have endeavoured to produce a useful handbook with easy to follow instructions and entertaining, accessible ideas.

Helen Sonnet

'What are we doing next time?'

This is a familiar question at the close of a club for people with a learning disability. In more than thirty years working with adults who often show challenging behaviour my *greatest* challenge has been to build a workable programme of activities for a group of these delightful individuals.

The boisterous eighteen-year-old can participate alongside an eighty-year-old with a walking frame. There is a need to extend and inspire autistic members, whilst including the non-communicating participant. Activities need to be affordable and safe, working within the limitations of help and space available.

It is, therefore, perhaps unsurprising (given the acknowledged confines) that there are few resource publications available in this rewarding sector. We are very well served with children's activity books, but the material in these is pictorially childish and therefore inappropriate for these special people, whose adult feelings should be respected.

This book is intended to provide ideas and activities for use in clubs or supported living homes. I have found each of these to be highly workable in our Gateway Club, a group of 35 sixteen to eighty-year-olds with very mixed mental and physical abilities. Whilst activity-based club nights can be exhausting for the leader, they do result in regular, keen attendance by the members and respect in the community when applying for grants or assistance.

Both I and my highly motivated group of helpers are amply rewarded for all our efforts when we see the enjoyment and pleasure that we are able to give to the members of our club.

Ann Taylor

HOW TO USE THIS BOOK

For easy access this book is divided into sections describing similar events. At the beginning of each section, you will find general information, hints and tips relating to the activities that follow.

At the start of each activity there is a box of specific information, and the key below explains the details given in these boxes.

L1, L2 and L3   This relates to the level of assistance required:

L1 =   Most participants will be able to manage this activity with a minimum level of assistance.

L2 =   Some participants will need assistance to participate in this activity.

L3 =   A high level of assistance is needed.

W/Ch =   This activity is suitable for wheelchair users.

V =   This activity involves a high volume of noise, which some participants may find distressing.

M =   This activity is messy, and participants may need to wear protective clothing.

R =   Reading skill may be required for this activity.

! =   there is a health and safety issue to be aware of, which will be specified.

Some activities also have diagrams and templates to assist you with the instructions.

Some of the activities may appear to be very labour-intensive – for example, you may have to make a large quantity of resources for a particular game. Don't be put off! Enlist the help of others to produce what is needed as, once resources have been made, they can be used again and again – especially if they have been laminated. In fact, a laminator is a really useful piece of equipment to have at your disposal. If your budget is insufficient to purchase one, you could consider a fundraising activity or even make an appeal in your local newspaper for donations. We have tried to make this book as comprehensive as possible, based on our experience and learnt wisdom. We hope all the additional advice we provide will ensure that you achieve success in all the activities that you undertake with your own group.

Finally, get stuck in and have *fun*!

COOKING

Where food is prepared and eaten by participants in an activity, there are a few health and safety issues that need to be addressed. Organization and safety are of paramount concern and the following guidelines will help you with these considerations.

It is always a good idea to advertise a cooking activity in advance as dietary requirements or food allergies may be an issue for some. (Participants who are unable to eat the items they have cooked can still take them home for others to enjoy.)

It is important to ensure that you have sufficient help in order to ensure a successful outcome. You will need to allocate the following jobs to your helpers:

- Chief cook – buys and prepares ingredients and gives instructions on the day.

- Pre-activity helpers – scrub tables and prepare the cooking area. Chairs can make a useful safety barrier to cordon off the cooking area.

- Preparation helper – collects participants together and ensures they are ready for cooking.

- Cookery helpers – work with participants to prepare ingredients and follow recipe processes.

- Baker – takes charge of the cooking process.

Participants will need easy access to washing facilities to ensure that their hands are clean before they begin to do any food preparation or cooking. It may be a good idea to place a couple of washing-up bowls, a liquid soap dispenser and towels on a table next to the food-preparation area.

Keep a kitchen roll handy to mop up spills and for people to use to wipe runny noses, etc.

Some participants may need to sit down during the food preparation and others may need additional assistance in reaching ingredients and utensils.

A suitable level of assistance and supervision is clearly essential where sharp knives or other potentially dangerous utensils are used during the preparation of the recipe. It may be advisable to demonstrate the safe handling of knives and remind the participants that utensils must remain on the chopping board when not in use. Forks can be used to hold one end of the food in place whilst the other end is being cut.

Be aware of any considerations specific to each recipe that might affect participants, e.g. onion vapour, (which can cause eyes to water), noise from food processors, the need to avoid licking of bowls that have contained raw eggs.

Make sure first-aiders are present in case of scalds, cuts or other accidents.

If you have sufficient help or time is short, it is very useful to weigh out and bag up the ingredients in advance in individual/group portions since this can be quite a lengthy process for people who have impaired mobility or understanding, and where you have forty or more participants.

Unless otherwise stated, the recipes we provide are intended for groups of six participants at a time.

Where whole group cooking is indicated, you could use a bell or whistle to gain quiet in order to give out each set of instructions.

SMALL CAKES

L2; W/Ch; M; ! – hot materials, ovens

Equipment

baking tray,	small cake-cases,	2 mixing bowls,
sieve,	cup,	fork,
wooden spoon,	scales,	dessertspoon,
teaspoon,	carry-home bags	

Ingredients (Makes 18 small cakes)

- 100g soft margarine or butter
- 100g caster sugar
- 2 eggs
- 100g self-raising flour

What to do

Pre-heat oven to 190°C/375°F/Gas mark 5. Allocate tasks to each participant as follows.

1. Lay out the cake-cases on the baking tray.
2. Put margarine into bowl.
3. Put sugar into bowl and mix with margarine. All cream together the margarine and sugar until smooth and fluffy.
4. Break eggs into cup, beat with fork, beat into mixture.

5. Sieve flour into second bowl, then fold the flour into the mixture.

6. Use the dessertspoon to scoop up the mixture and scrape into two cake-cases with the teaspoon (half fill each cake-case). All take a turn to fill a cake-case.

7. Bake in oven for approx. 10–15 minutes until golden brown.

8. Leave to cool and cover tops with water icing and cake decorations.

Variations

Add 50g of chocolate chips or currants to the mixture before filling the cake-cases.

PIZZA

L3; W/Ch; M; ! – hot items, oven, sharp utensils

Equipment

cheese grater	4 chopping boards or plates
2 large spoons	1 teaspoon
knife for spreading	4 vegetable knives
round baking tin	carry-home bags or paper plates
plate	

Ingredients per group

- 1 large shop-bought pizza base
- 250ml pre-cooked tomato paste (see options)

Option 1:

- onion (large)
- teaspoon of herbs
- carton of creamed tomato

Option 2:

- tube of tomato purée
- pinch of mixed herbs
- finely chopped onion

- 100g cheese
- assortment of toppings such as ham, pepperoni, mushrooms, peppers, red onion, tinned sweetcorn.

Paste option 1

This has the better taste but will need preparing prior to the cooking session. Chop and fry one large onion. Add 2 teaspoons of mixed herbs and a carton of creamed tomato. Boil until the mixture achieves a thickened consistency, season to taste. This quantity will cover 3 pizzas.

Paste option 2

A tube of concentrated tomato purée makes a quick and easy paste. You can then sprinkle over it a pinch of mixed herbs and finely chopped onion if required.

What to do

Pre-heat oven to 180°C/350°F/Gas mark 4. Allocate one of the following tasks to each of the participants.

1. Grate cheese.
2. Spread paste mixture onto base.
3. Chop or slice topping ingredients of choice (x4 participants).
4. Each participant puts on a spoonful of cheese and ingredients.
5. Top with any remaining cheese to retain moisture.
6. Cook for 20 minutes or until cheese is golden brown.
7. Leave to cool slightly and then slice.

FLAPJACKS

L2; W/Ch; M; ! – oven

Equipment

12-inch by 9-inch baking tray (this size tray will make 16–20 portions)

mixing bowl and wooden spoon

baking parchment

wire rack

carry-home bags

Ingredients

- 6oz/180g soft margarine or butter
- 6oz/180g soft brown sugar
- 8oz/210g rolled oats
- 1 tablespoon golden syrup
- small pinch of salt.

What to do

Pre-heat oven to 170°C/ 325°F/Gas mark 3. Allocate one of the following tasks to each participant.

1. Line the baking tray with the parchment.

2. Put the margarine into the bowl.

3. Put the sugar into the bowl and mix with the margarine. All take a turn to stir.

4. Put in the syrup, rolled oats and pinch of salt and stir mixture. All take a turn to stir.

5. Turn the mixture into the baking tray.

6. Spread the mixture evenly over the tray.

7. Place in the pre-heated oven and bake for 25 minutes or until golden brown.

8. Whilst warm, cut the flapjack into portions and place on a wire rack to cool.

COOKIES

L2; W/Ch; M; ! – oven

Equipment

2 mixing bowls	spatula/scraper
sieve	baking parchment
2 wooden spoons	baking tray
cup	scales if ingredients are not pre-weighed
fork	carry-home bags

Ingredients (Makes 12 cookies)

- 50g soft margarine
- 100g sugar
- 1 egg
- 100g self-raising flour
- 50g flavouring, e.g. chocolate chips, coconut, glacé-cherry pieces, currants.

What to do

Pre-heat oven to 190°C/375°F/Gas mark 5. Line baking tray with parchment. Number participants 1–6. Allocate tasks as follows.

1. Place magerine in bowl.
2. Place sugar in same bowl.

3. Stir mixture together.

4. Break egg into cup.

5. Beat egg with fork.

6. Add egg to mixture and stir.

All have a turn at beating

1. Sieve flour into dry bowl.

2. Add flavouring to mixture in first bowl.

3. Stir flavouring into mixture.

4. Add sieved flour to the mixture.

5. Stir everything together.

All have a stir

6. Spoon the first two spoonfuls (walnut-sized) onto lined tray.

All take a turn.

7. Bake in centre of oven for 7 to 10 minutes until golden brown.

BONFIRE CAKES

> L3; W/Ch; M; ! – boiling water

All the members can make this recipe together, but for management purposes there should be a maximum of six participants to a table along with one helper. A designated 'baker' is in charge of melting the bowls of chocolate over pans of hot water. The baker also melts the chocolate for the All-Bran topping. It may be helpful to have someone in the centre of the room to call out instructions for all the participants.

Equipment

kettle or microwave	chief cook's large bowl
per group: spoon, cups for icing	saucepan and large bowl to stand it in
large spoon	6 teaspoons
6 cardboard discs or CDs	6 squares of foil
roll of dispenser sellotape	strips of paper for names
wet kitchen roll for mucky fingers	carry-home bags

Ingredients (Makes 6 cakes)

- 200g cooking chocolate

- 200g Rice Krispies

- 100g All-Bran

- water icing in various flame colours, e.g. white, red, yellow, orange made up in egg-cup size containers to the consistency of salad cream.

What to do

1. All participants help to break the chocolate bars into chunks and place in bowls for the 'baker'. (The baker needs to keep back 3 chunks from each group for the topping.)

2. Whilst the 'baker' is melting the chocolate, the participants cover their CD in foil, held in place with sellotape. Attach a protruding name slip to each disc.

3. The participants add Rice Krispies to their bowls of melted chocolate and take turns to stir. Group helpers oversee dividing the mixture between the covered discs. The participants use their fingers to pile up the mixture into a mound.

4. The participants use teaspoons to drizzle coloured icing over their mounds of chocolate mixture. This will create the internal fire. The baker melts the chocolate for the topping and adds the All-Bran.

5. The All-bran topping is divided between the participants bowls. It is then shared between the participants and they arrange the bran sticks over their bonfire mound.

6. More icing can be drizzled over the top of the bonfire and it is then placed somewhere cold to set. When they are set, the bonfire cakes can be cut into wedges to show the 'fire' inside.

ROCK BUNS

L2; W/Ch; M; ! – oven

Equipment

2 mixing bowls	carry-home bags
2 wooden spoons	sieve
cup	teaspoon
spatula/scraper	fork
2 baking trays	baking parchment

Ingredients (Makes around 12 large buns)

- 100g soft margarine
- 200g self-raising flour
- 1 teaspoon of mixed spice
- 100g mixed fruit with peel
- 1 egg
- 50 ml milk (approx).

What to do

Preheat oven to 200°C/180°F/Gas mark 6. Number participants 1–6. Allocate tasks as follows.

1. Tip flour into sieve over one mixing bowl.

2. Add mixed spice.

3. Sieve flour by pressing with wooden spoon.

4. Put margarine into second bowl.

5. Add sieved flour to margarine.

6. Rub margarine and flour together (a helper can demonstrate this technique) until it resembles fine breadcrumbs.

All take a turn

1. Add dried fruit.

2. Stir dried fruit into the mixture.

3. Break egg into cup.

4. Beat egg with fork.

5. Add egg to mixture.

6. Add milk to mixture and stir.

All take a turn at stirring the mixture

7. Each participant can spoon two small heaps of the mixture onto the baking tray.

8. Cook for 7–8 minutes until golden.

FRUIT PUNCH

L2; W/Ch; M; ! – sharp utensils,
choking on small pieces of fruit

This is a great activity to do while waiting for something else to happen, e.g. BBQ food to cook or as a pre-runner to an awards evening. Using diet lemonade makes it a healthier option.

Equipment

New washing-up bowl   chopping boards

vegetable knives and forks   cup or ladle

long-handled kitchen spoon to mix

Ingredients (Makes about 50 servings)

- 4 litres of a selection of fruit juices such as orange, pineapple, apple, or cranberry

- 4 litres diet lemonade

- 1 litre water

- assortment fresh fruit such as red and green apples, oranges, kiwi fruit and grapes

- mint leaves to serve.

What to do

1. Divide the participants into three teams:

    - one to wash fruit, remove inedible peel and de-seed

- one to chop fruit, and

- a smaller group to add liquid ingredients and mix. Helpers can cut fruit into quarters to enable more participants to be involved more easily in the chopping activity. Helpers need to direct chopping activity to ensure safety procedures are observed.

2. The fruit is cut into thin slices and placed into the bowl.

3. The mixing team adds the fruit juice first in order to prevent browning of apples.

4. Add the water and stir gently.

5. Just prior to serving, add the lemonade and float sprigs of mint on on the surface.

6. Scoop out punch with a cup or ladle and serve into glasses. Have spoons ready for those who would prefer to eat the fruit before drinking the punch.

VEGETABLE SOUP

L3; W/Ch; V; ! – sharp utensils, hot pans,
hot liquids, food-processor blade

This cookery session can be done as a whole-group activity. The chief cook and helpers can oversee the food handling, with several participants chopping vegetables at a time (a 1:1 or 2:1 ratio is advisable for chopping.) A display table of whole vegetables nearby can be an educating experience. However, supervision is necessary, otherwise vegetables might be added – dirt, skins and all!

Equipment

1 chopping board or plate per cook

1 large saucepan (per 10 participants) or pressure cooker

forks, assorted knives, peelers and scrubbing utensils

4 bowls for washing peelings and chopped vegetables

tasting spoons	second large saucepan
food processor	wooden spoon
jug	hot plate or cooker
kettle	carry-home containers

Ingredients (this quantity will make around 10 servings)

- 8 mixed vegetables such as swedes, potatoes, pumpkin (to give the soup some body), carrots (good for colour), onions, leeks, celery (to give soup flavour), parsnips, turnips, marrow, courgettes

- 1 vegetable stock cube
- 1 tsp mixed herbs
- 500 ml boiling water
- 3 tablespoons evaporated milk or cream (optional)
- salt and pepper to taste
- bread rolls
- butter/low fat spread.

What to do

1. Each participant can choose a vegetable for the pot and scrub or peel that vegetable as appropriate.

2. Helper cuts vegetable into finger-sized portions for cook to chop into small pieces and place into one of the vegetable bowls.

3. Add stock cube and chopped vegetables to saucepan or pressure cooker (if using pressure cooker add less water and cook for 10 minutes).

4. Cover vegetables with boiling water and simmer for about 25 minutes, until soft.

5. Liquidise in a food processor, or use a potato masher.

6. Transfer into the clean saucepan, and add water to give required consistency.

7. Cooks can use teaspoons to taste the soup and decide if salt and pepper are required. (remind cooks not to put their teaspoons back into the soup once they've tasted it using them).

8. Whilst the soup is being cooked and processed, the participants can butter the bread rolls to go with it.

ARTS AND CRAFTS

Making things is always a popular past-time, and it is useful to collect a supply of suitable resources for this – many of which can be obtained by recycling materials such as old cards, pictures, scraps of material, wool and ribbon. You will also need various glues – PVA, solvent-free UHU, glue sticks and sellotape – a stapler, and round-ended scissors. If your budget allows, it can be useful to have a selection of card and coloured and metallic paper (a roll of lining wallpaper is an inexpensive source of paper), shells, sequins and feathers. Coloured pencils, thick and thin paint brushes, paint in primary colours, black and white, wax crayons and felt-tip pens should complete your basic supplies.

If you have sufficient space, you can also keep in store a variety of containers such as yoghurt pots, polystyrene cups, jar lids for holding glue or paint, and cereal boxes. Margarine pots make useful containers in which to stand water jars to prevent spillage, though it is always a good idea to keep a roll of kitchen paper handy anyway for mopping up and wiping things clean. A stack of newspapers should be kept to protect table tops from paint, glue, etc.

'Glue pads' offer an easy way to stick items. To make one, you need to line a flat-bottomed tray, e.g. the lid of an ice-cream tub, with a damp piece of fabric (a piece of J-cloth is ideal). Onto this you pour a tablespoonful of PVA glue and spread it over the cloth with your fingers or the back of a spoon. Flip the piece of cloth over and smooth it flat. The glue seeps through the fabric when pressed down on. The pad is ready to use. Place the items to be glued onto the cloth and press them on to it gently. Lift them off and place them onto the required site.

Sometimes a general plea for art materials can bring in a stock of useful supplies, but you will probably find that you need to buy specific materials from time to time. Craft shops can be very expensive, whereas catalogue/mail order companies (see our recommendations below) offer a wide range of resources at more affordable prices, though you will have to plan your ordering to allow time for deliveries. The two companies that we use are:

Baker Ross: Baker Ross Limited, Freepost ND995, London, E17 6BR. Online: www.bakerross.co.uk
Can be ordered direct – great for easy-to-use craft kits and smaller amounts of clay, glues, paper, scissors, pens, calendar tabs, and so on.

GLS Educational Supplies: GLS Educational Supplies, 1 Mollison Avenue, Enfield, EN3 7XQ. Online: www.glsed.co.uk
Requires the setting up of an account; comprehensive mail-order catalogue covering most craft needs, games, music, catering equipment, and disposable aprons.

CHRISTMAS NAME-PLAQUES

L2, W/Ch; ! – scissors, small items,
read spray paint instructions before use

Equipment

gold and silver card which has been cut into an oval shape about 20–25cm long by 15cm deep (for 'plaque'), (you can either buy this or prepare your own using stiff corrugated cardboard from a box or other thick card, which you cover with spray paint), wool, hole puncher, Christmas pot-pourri selection, Christmas sequin selection, tinsel, PVA glue and UHU for the larger decorations, scissors, computer-generated names of participants (this looks even better if you cut round the name with pinking shears or other scissors with shaped blades).

What to do

1. Prepare one or two tables with the equipment, depending on the number of helpers available.

2. Invite the participants, a few at a time, to come to the tables and make their plaques.

3. Participants should be shown how to glue their names onto the plaque and decorate the surrounding space.

4. The plaque is completed by punching holes at the top and threading through a length of wool or ribbon for hanging.

SHELL POTS

> L2; W/Ch; M; ! – shells

Equipment

polystyrene cups (you can use plastic cups, but they are not as sturdy), art mâché (powdered paper and glue, available from the stockists we have named), assortment of small shells (if you have collected these from a beach, it is a good idea to wash them in disinfectant before use), PVA glue, gold and silver powder paint, paper name tags.

What to do

1. Prepare one or two tables with the equipment, depending on the number of helpers available.

2. Invite a few participants at a time to the tables to make their pots.

3. Demonstrate holding the cup by placing the left fist inside, this helps to keep the sides rigid.

4. Give the participants a lump of art mâché, about the size of a small apple.

5. Show them how to work the mâché around the outside of the cup, until the sides are covered. Leave the base free.

6. Press small shells into the mâché to decorate, using PVA glue to aid adherence.

7. Participants then put their finger into the gold or silver paint and press them onto the art mâché, between the shells. This gives an attractive mottled effect.

8. Leave the cups to dry upside down, alongside a name tag (cups will take several days to fully dry out).

CALENDARS

L1; W/Ch; ! – scissors

Equipment

A4 card, selection of pictures of animals, country scenes, cartoon characters, etc. (these can be old cards or taken from sources such as magazines, wrapping paper, or old calendar pictures), scissors, glue sticks, wool or ribbon, hole puncher, calendar tabs.

What to do

1. Prepare one or two tables with the equipment, depending on the number of helpers available.

2. Invite the participants a few at a time to the table.

3. Explain that they are going to decorate the top half of the A4 piece of card with one or more pictures of their choice and add a calendar tab to the bottom half.

4. Punch two holes at the top of the card and thread with wool or ribbon for hanging.

5. Write the participants' names on the back of their cards.

WAX WASH PAINTING

L1; W/Ch; R; M

Equipment

A4 paper (not too absorbent and one sheet for every participant), yellow or white wax crayons or candles, brusho or diluted ready-mixed paint (a dark colour such as blue or purple is preferable), paint brushes, plastic trays for the brusho/paint.

What to do

1. Prepare one or two tables with the equipment, depending on the number of helpers available.

2. Invite the participants, a few at a time, to the tables.

3. Write their names onto the back of their pieces of paper.

4. Demonstrate drawing a pattern or object on the paper with the wax crayons or candles. Emphasize the need to press firmly with the crayon and to repeat lines several times. Ask them to do the same, creating their own design on their piece of paper.

5. They should then brush over their paper with the paint or brusho and leave to dry.

6. Those participants with adequate literacy skills can try writing 'secret messages' to other group members using a white candle on white paper. The recipient of the message paints over the wax to reveal what has been written!

HANGING DECORATION

(sequins sandwiched between sticky-backed plastic)

L3; W/Ch; ! – scissors; small items

Equipment

Cut out two rectangles from a roll of sticky-backed plastic (as used for covering books) for each participant. One rectangle should measure 18 x 36cms and the other 15 x 30cms, scissors, wool or ribbon, sequins, permanent marker. (You can prepare the sticky-backed plastic with the required templates prior to the session to save time.)

What to do

1. Prepare one or two tables with equipment, depending on the number of helpers available.

2. Invite the participants, a few at a time, to the tables.

3. Fold both rectangles of sticky-backed plastic in half to form squares.

4. Using the permanent marker, draw a circle on the plastic surface of one half of the larger square.

5. Draw a tab on one edge of the circle for hanging the decoration up by.

6. Gently ease one corner of backing paper away from the sticky surface on the half containing the drawn circle and fold to allow for easy peeling.

7. Help the participant to peel away the backing paper to the half-way mark.

8. They should then place sequins in a pattern of their choice onto the sticky surface.

9. The remaining half of the backing paper is then peeled away, and the two sticky surfaces brought together to sandwich the sequins in between. The participants cut out the drawn circle with its tab.

10. Using the permanent marker, draw a circle on the plastic surface of one half of the smaller square.

11. Starting at one edge of the circle, draw a spiral of concentric circles until you reach the centre of the circle.

12. Gently ease one corner of the backing paper away from the sticky surface on the half containing the drawn pattern.

13. Help the participant to peel away the backing paper.

14. They place sequins in a pattern of their choice *between* the drawn lines.

15. The remaining half of the backing paper is then peeled away and the two sticky surfaces brought together to sandwich the sequins in between.

16. The participants cut out the drawn circle and then cut along the spiralling line to the centre of the circle to make a twirler.

17. Make a hole in the tab of the larger circle and thread through wool for hanging.

18. Attach the twirler to the larger circle with a short, single length of wool.

PASTA CANDLE-HOLDERS

L2; W/Ch! (read spray paint instructions before use)

Equipment

old CDs	PVA glue
air-drying clay	gold/silver spray paint
various pasta shapes	candle

What to do

1. Prepare one or two tables with equipment, depending on the number of helpers available.

2. Invite the participants a few at a time, to come to the tables.

3. Each participant is given a CD and a lump of clay the size of a small apple.

4. Ask them to place the clay in the centre of the CD, pushing the candle firmly into the centre of the ball and press in pasta shapes around the sides of the clay, using PVA glue to aid adherence.

5. When the clay has dried out, the art work is sprayed gold/silver.

PHOTO FRAMES

L2; W/Ch; M

There are three options for this activity, and you can choose to do just one or more:

- Option 1. The frames have a printed border made from a stamp or object dipped in paint

- Option 2. The frames are covered in pot-pourri

- Option 3. The frames are covered in small pasta shapes and spray-painted.

Equipment

Photo frames, plus a backing card. (To make your own, cut two pieces of card 1.5 cms larger than the photo size for each frame. Cut out a window with a 2-cm frame from one piece of card and retain the insert. Put a thin line of glue around *three* edges of the other backing card then position the frame on top. Use the insert to make a stand, by bending back 1-cm tabs on the furthest ends and gluing these to the back.)

- Option 1. Stamps and ink pads, or shape for printing and ready mixed paint

- Option 2. A selection of pot-pourri containing small items, PVA glue

- Option 3. Small pasta shapes, PVA glue, spray paint. digital camera, card-reading or specialist photo printer.

What to do

1. Prepare one or two tables with equipment, depending on the number of helpers available.

2. Invite the participants, a few at a time to the tables.

3. Each participant should be helped to decorate a photo frame with the available equipment.

4. Write their names on the back of the frames.

5. Meanwhile, a helper takes a photo of each member with the digital camera. As this is a time-consuming process, you need to start as early as possible, or if you prefer, take the pictures and print out the photos prior to the session.

6. When the photos are ready, slip them into the frame through the open edge.

DOOR-HANDLE HANGERS

L2; W/Ch; ! – scissors

Equipment

the template (shown in Figure 1), rectangles of card large enough to fit the template, scissors. (Prepare several templates in advance of the session.)

What to do

1. Prepare one or two tables with the equipment, depending on the number of helpers available.

2. Invite the participants, a few at a time, to the tables.

3. Ask the participants to draw and cut out the card (with help if necessary), using the template.

4. Participants should choose a message to write on their door hanger. This could be a useful exercise in communications, but be aware that conflicting issues of privacy versus welfare may arise and you will need to deal with these. For example, if the message says 'Keep Out', this may not be applicable to carers.

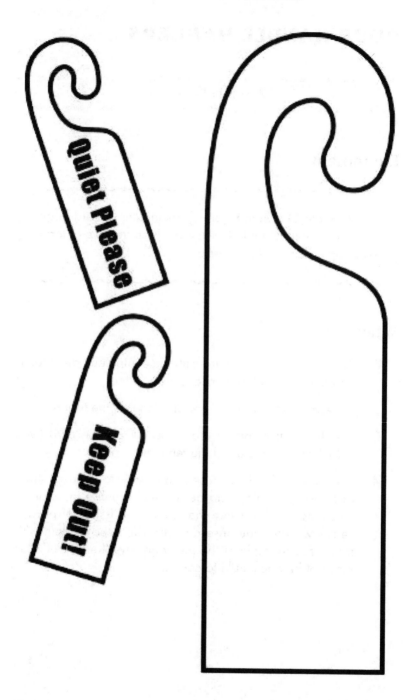

Figure 1

NAME BADGES

L2; W/Ch; ! – sharp objects

Equipment

Stiff cardboard rectangles (you can cut 4 from an A4 sheet of card), large safety pins, duct tape, pre-prepared cut out symbols of men and women in metallic paper, glue pads for the metallic paper, coloured felt-tip pens, computer-generated names.

What to do

1. Prepare one or two tables with equipment, depending on the help available.

2. Invite participants, a few at a time, to the tables.

3. Make sure each participant has a piece of card and a male or female symbol according to their own gender, which they glue onto the card alongside their name.

4. They should then be asked to think of something that they like and draw this or a representative symbol onto their card, e.g. a dog, the letter 'G' (for Gateway Club), a sun, a glass of beer, a book. Group members who cannot read can usually recognize a symbol. Encourage the participants to think of a symbol that others would associate with them.

5. Attach a safety pin to the back of the card with duct tape.

6. You can then, if you want, get the participants to hold a name badge show and take turns to parade in front of everyone, wearing their name tag.

ART COMPETITION

Art competitions are a popular way of generating an opportunity for the members of your organization to show off and feel proud of their own work. You can give an additional boost to their self-esteem if you can persuade a local artist to act as a judge. (Someone from the Society of Disabled Artists would be sympathetic to the participants' special needs. Their contact details are: SODA, Bramfield House, Church Road, Little Ellingham, Norfolk NR17 1JN, telephone 01953 850381.)

Start by preparing an A5 leaflet advertising the competition that they can take home with them. This will help them and their carers to remember the event.

The leaflet needs to contain the following information:

- date of competition

- number of entries allowed, e.g. 3

- ideas for entries, e.g. paintings, sculptures, drawings, sewing, models, pots, colouring in, computer designs

- who will be judging the entries

- what the prizes are

- a contact phone number for further information.

Make sure that you give plenty of notice of the event and provide several opportunities for those members who do not have access to art materials at home to create an entry.

Borrow or make display boards for pictures and drape tables for 3-D objects. Some suggested categories are:

- painting and drawing

- pots and sculptures

- created pictures, e.g. collages, greetings cards

- other, e.g. sewing, knitting, photos, computer-generated work.

It is important to ensure a good-quality exhibition so that you reward participants for their efforts. Post-it labels can be used for showing First, Second and Third placings and for judges' comments.

You may be able to interest the local press in running a feature on the competition – the participants will love to see their pictures in the paper.

PARTY GAMES

Most people enjoy playing party games and people with learning disabilities are no exception. The selection included here are games that we play regularly, and they are always popular and well supported – although you may find a few members will prefer to watch rather than participate.

Prepare your room to create maximum space and ensure safety. Make sure you sequence the games in order to minimize furniture movement, e.g. use chairs for a seated circle after Musical Chairs. A sedentary game following food consumption is advisable in order to allow people's food to settle and check that there are no spillages on the floor, making it slippery and dangerous.

A prize tray is appreciated by the winners, who should be able to choose from a selection of items such as pens, coloured pencils, hair ties, fruit, sweets, colouring books, lip salve and soft toys.

If you are playing team games, the party-goers can be greeted as they enter with a team coloured welcome badge, to save time. Remember to be aware of those members who would prefer just to watch.

ADULT MUSICAL CHAIRS

L2; W/Ch; V! – jostling may lead to falls

Equipment

A line of chairs facing in alternate directions, one for each of the men present, a CD of music and a CD player.

What to do

1. The men sit on the chairs.

2. The music starts and the women walk around the line of chairs in a clockwise direction.

3. When the music stops, the women must find a lap to perch on.

4. After each turn, one or two chairs are removed from either end of the row.

5. Any woman without a lap to perch on when the music stops next is out.

6. This continues until there is a winner, then the roles are reversed and the women sit on the chairs.

If you have a large number of wheelchair users, they can still play a version of musical chairs separately.

1. Large coloured circles are drawn onto separate sheets of A4 paper and laid out in a row.

2. Helpers push the wheelchairs around the row of circles while the music is playing and when it stops, they must find a spot for the wheelchair to stand on.

3. After each turn, one or two spots are removed from either end.

BALLOON RACE

L2; W/Ch; V; ! – be aware of any mobility problems

Equipment

Balloons (if participants are frightened of balloons bursting, you can use scrunched up balls of tissue paper instead), enough newspapers for each participant. These should be rolled up and sellotaped so they stay in the roll, forming a kind of bat.

What to do

1. Participants stand in a line at one end of the room facing the opposite end of the room.

2. They are each given a rolled and sellotaped newspaper to hold and a balloon is placed on the floor at their feet.

3. On the command 'Go', the participants flap the newspaper bat back and forth to create a draught in order to waft the balloon to the opposite end of the room.

4. The first one there is the winner. Participants are not allowed to hit the balloon with the newspaper.

You could also have a relay balloon race or a knockout competition with heats and a final.

Wheelchair users will need to be given a longer rolled up newspaper.

MUSICAL HATS

L2; W/Ch V; ! – be aware of any mobility problems

Equipment

A selection of hats (if possible try and provide one for each of the participants), a CD of music and a CD player.

What to do

1. Place several tables together to make one long table in the centre of the room. Ensure there is sufficient space for the participants to walk around it.

2. Spread the hats out on the table surface.

3. The participants should be asked to walk round the table in a clockwise direction while the music is playing.

4. When the music stops, the participants must find a hat and put it on their head. Anyone without a hat is out.

5. Have a practice run to start with, where everyone has a hat and then remove one or two each time until you have a winner.

NOVELTY RACES
1. THE 'FIND IT' RACE

L2; W/Ch; ! – scissors

Equipment

Large prepared (see below) sheets of A3 paper (or a roll of old wallpaper), glue sticks, scissors, a selection of magazines.

What to do

1. Divide one large sheet of paper into several boxes (at least 10cm square).

2. At the top of each box, write an item or colour likely to be found in the magazines, e.g. a car, a baby, a fruit, the colour blue, a cake, a smiling face, a dog, a hat, a flower, a tree, a dress, a pair of glasses, a house, some jewellery, a shoe.

3. Divide the participants into teams and allocate a table to each team. Try and ensure a similar level of ability and skills in each team. Each table of participants will need a prepared sheet of items to find, scissors, glue stick and several magazines.

4. On the command 'Go', the members of each team look through the magazines to try and locate one of the items named.

5. They then cut this out and stick it in the appropriate box on their sheet of paper. It may be a good idea to suggest that each team member looks for a different item to save time.

6. The team that completes all their boxes first is the winner.

2. THE 'FIND THE PERSON' RACE

This activity is similar to the one above.

1. Before the session, cut out a selection of pictures of people from magazines. You will need at least ten for each table.

2. Cut each figure into three: head, torso and legs.

3. Jumble the body parts up and place in the centre of the table.

4. Each table of participants needs a large sheet of plain paper and a glue stick.

5. On the command 'Go', the participants look through the body parts to find the ones that match. They assemble the head, torso and legs and glue them onto their paper.

6. The first team to correctly assemble their figures is the winner.

WHAT'S IN THE CUSHION CASE?

L1; W/Ch

Equipment

A cushion case, a variety of objects such as a toothbrush, a ball of wool, a small roll of sellotape, a sponge, a plastic cup, a packet of crisps, an orange, a battery, a peg and a spoon. Try and ensure that there are enough objects for everyone participating to have a guess.

What to do

1. Before the session, fill one or more cushion cases with about ten objects and close the zip.

2. Ask the participants to sit in a circle.

3. The first participant is handed the cushion case and is allowed to feel the objects inside.

4. The remaining players clap their hands together ten times, at the end of which the person holding the cushion case must try and guess one (only) object hidden inside.

5. If the guess is correct, the leader removes that object and the cushion case is passed to the next player.

6. The procedure is repeated for each player.

7. If after ten claps a player is unable to hazard a guess, the case is passed on to the next participant.

8. When the objects in the case have all been removed, the leader either introduces a new cushion case or fills the original one with a new set of objects.

GRANNY'S SHOPPING RELAY

L2; W/Ch; V; ! – be aware of any mobility problems

Equipment

A selection of lightweight shopping items, e.g. empty cereal packet, empty tea packet, packet of biscuits, small pot of herbs, small packet of tissues, packet of pencils, small sellotape-dispenser, cards, envelopes, carrots, onions. You will need sufficient items for each player to collect one and a shopping bag for each team. To add to the fun, try and have a shawl and hat for each team as well.

What to do

1. Put the participants into teams at one end of the room. Try and divide them equally in terms of mobility.

2. Place the shopping items on tables at the other end of the room. (Make sure that each table has the same or similar items.)

3. The first player in each team puts on the hat and shawl and carries the shopping basket.

4. He or she proceeds to the other end of the room and selects one item of shopping to go into the bag.

5. They then return as quickly as possible and pass the hat, shawl and bag to the next player, who repeats the process.

6. The winning team is the first to have all players collect an item of shopping, but let all the teams finish, so that everyone has a turn.

DOG BONES

L2; W/Ch; V; ! – be aware of mobility problems

Equipment

Makes some 'bones' from white card (you will need to prepare around 12 bones for each pair of players). On one side of the bones write an instruction such as: under chin, between 2 fingers, between thumb and elbow, between knees, behind ear, between teeth, between shoulder and ear, under arms, choose where it goes and give to another pair to hold.

What to do

1. Invite the players to find a partner. In each pair, one is the dog and must hold the bones (a suitable role for wheelchair users) and the other is the dresser.

2. The pairs stand in a large circle, surrounded by the audience (any members who prefer to play), leaving the centre space empty.

3. Place the bones face on the floor in the centre space.

4. On the command 'Go', all the dressers run into the centre and picks up one (only) bone.

5. The dresser takes the bone to the dog who must hold the bone according to the instruction written. The dresser can place the bone in the correct position for the dog if necessary.

6. The dresser then collects another bone.

7. The game continues in this fashion for several minutes until you can see that the dogs are full to overflowing with bones.

8. Each dog counts how many bones they have been able to hold, without dropping.

9. The dog with the most and their dresser are the winners.

10. Instruct the dressers to stand behind the dogs so that the audience has a good view of the action.

GENERAL GAMES

A general games evening is fun for all involved, whether as participants or spectators. Some games such as static hockey are intended as whole-club activities, but other games (requiring less space and with fewer participants) can be grouped together as a session.

You will need to ensure that sufficient helpers are available to organize and run each activity and take particular care in safely positioning any games where items are being propelled.

Individual score-cards are a good idea for a multiple games session. The club members' names can be entered onto their cards prior to commencement. They then carry their cards with them for the session and their scores are entered after each event.

Alternatively, each game can have a large mark-sheet of paper displayed alongside the activity. The helper can enter the name of the participant and their score after each turn.

If you can, buy some inexpensive medals to award, or print out certificates. At the very least, gather all the participants together at the end of the session to give a round of applause to the winners of each game.

If your budget is very limited, you could approach schools or other social organizations to see if you could borrow their equipment – for example, inflatable netball stands.

STATIC HOCKEY

L2; W/Ch; V

Equipment

Chairs, balloons, rolled and taped newspaper bats.

What to do

1. Divide the participants into two teams. Try and select the teams so that they are evenly matched physically.

2. The teams should sit in alternate rows of chairs, facing in opposite directions (see Figure 2).

3. Create a goal at either end of the playing area using chairs to mark the goal posts.

4. A helper throws a blown-up balloon into the middle of the formation.

5. The participants use their newspaper bats to hit the balloon towards their opponent's goal, passing it along the room to their team members.

You will need helpers to keep a tally of the goals for each team. The helpers can also remind participants in which direction to hit the balloon, and to stay seated during play.

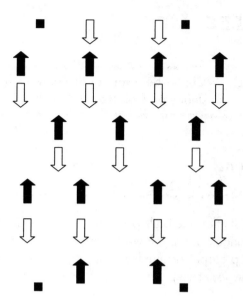

Figure 2

SKITTLES

L1; W/Ch; ! – be aware of any player who is
unsteady on their feet and might fall

Equipment

A set of skittles and balls (you can use plastic drinks bottles
and sponge balls as a low-cost alternative), masking tape,
rolled-up carpet or blankets. (Sponge balls are available
from any toy shop.)

What to do

1. Create a skittle alley using the rolled-up carpet or blankets
    to provide the boundary and to keep the balls from roll-
    ing away.

2. Mark the position of the skittles on the floor using mask-
    ing tape to ensure that they are placed correctly after each
    turn.

3. Mark three lines with the masking tape at varying intervals
    from the skittles to denote where the participants must
    stand to take their throw, according to their physical abil-
    ity. Those with the greatest mobility problems stand on the
    line nearest to the skittles.

4. Each participant has three throws and the number of skit-
    tles they have knocked down is recorded on their score-
    card or the mark-sheet.

NETBALL

L1; W/Ch; ! – be aware of any player who is
unsteady on their feet and might fall

Equipment

Inflatable netball stand, (if you are unable to buy or borrow
a stand, you can use a cardboard box with the top and
bottom removed, taped to a hook on the back of a door),
six balls, masking tape.

What to do

1. Ensure that you position the net away from any thorough-
   fare where passers by could be hit by the ball.

2. Mark three positions using the masking tape at varying
   distances from the 'net' to denote the playing positions
   according to the participants' physical ability. Those with
   the greatest mobility problems stand on the line nearest
   to the 'net'.

3. You may also want to lower the 'net' for wheelchair
   users.

4. Each player has six throws and the number of balls they
   throw through the net is recorded on their score-cards or
   the mark-sheet.

DARTS

L1; W/Ch; ! – be aware of any player who is unsteady
on their feet and might fall, beware of flying darts

Equipment

Safety dartboard (these can be purchased from catalogues or toyshops and are not particularly expensive) and
darts, masking tape.

What to do

1. Place your dartboard in a corner or position a barricade
   of chairs around the area to ensure that no one walks in
   front of the players.

2. Mark three lines with the masking tape at varying distances from the dartboard to denote the playing positions
   according to the participants' physical ability. Those with
   greatest mobility problems stand on the line nearest the
   board. You may also want to lower the board for wheelchair users.

3. Each player throws six darts and their total score is recorded on their score-card or the mark-sheet.

TOSS A BEAN BAG

L1; W/Ch; ! – be aware of any player who is
unsteady on their feet and might fall

Equipment

6 medium-sized plant pots,

6 large stones,

6 bean bags/balls,

masking tape.

What to do

1. Arrange the flower pots in a formation of three rows, with three at the front, two in the second row and one in the third row.

2. Write a score on the front of each pot, e.g. 5 on the front pots, 10 on the pots in the second row, and 20 on the furthest pot.

3. Place a large stone in each pot to stop it from being knocked over during play.

4. Mark three lines with the masking tape at varying distances from the pots to denote the playing positions according to the participants' physical ability. Those with greatest mobility problems stand on the line nearest the pots.

5. Each player has six throws, and their total score is recorded on their score-card or the mark-sheet.

GOAL SCORING

L1; ! – be aware of any player who is
unsteady on their feet and might fall

Equipment

Inflatable goal (or you can make one using a table on its side and garden netting: the top of the table acts as the back of the net and the garden netting, draped around the legs, forms the sides) 5 large sponge balls or other indoor friendly balls, masking tape.

What to do

1. Position the goal against a wall to reduce the risk of passers-by being hit by a ball.

2. Mark three lines with the masking tape at varying distances from the goal mouth to denote the playing positions according to physical ability. Those with greatest mobility problems stand on the line nearest the goal.

3. Each player has five shots at goal and their score is recorded on their score-card or the mark-sheet.

HOOPLA

L1; W/Ch; ! – be aware of any player who is unsteady
on their feet and might fall, beware of flying hoops

Equipment

Hoopla rings (if you are unable to buy or borrow any, you
can make some from card), bottles filled with water, masking tape, table.

What to do

1. Arrange the bottles in rows on a table top and give each a
    score. The bottles nearest the front have the lowest score
    and the bottles furthest away, the highest.

2. Mark three lines with the masking tape at varying distances
    from the table to denote the playing positions according
    to the participants' physical ability. Those with greatest
    mobility problems stand on the line nearest the table.

3. Each player has five rings to throw and their total score
    is recorded on their score-card or the mark-sheet. It may
    be advisable to demonstrate a suitable throwing action in
    order to avoid potentially dangerous under-arm throws.

COMPUTER GAMES

L1; W/Ch; ! – there may be mobility considerations;
be careful where electric wires are positioned;
be aware that some games can be problematic
for any participants suffering from epilepsy

Many games are available where more than the fingers can be exercised.

The 'Tony Hawk' series of skateboarding moves is ideal for all players, from the random button presser to a competent player. The games last a maximum of two minutes, but some need to be screened for violence.

Those with the capacity to add an eye toy to the computer can choose a game marked 'Eye Toy' to provide a physical input. (The Eye Toy is a colour digital camera device, similar to a webcam, for the PlayStation 2. The technology uses computer vision and gesture recognition to process images taken by the camera. This allows players to interact with games using motion, colour detection and sound, through its built-in microphone. (Wikipedia)) Whilst some have the players leaping around, many are suitable for hand movements while sitting in a chair.

PICTURE BINGO

L2; W/Ch

Equipment

Prior to the session, you will need to prepare a complete set of picture cards for the caller and bingo cards for the participants, using the illustrations in Figure 3 copy out and cut into individual pictures. (You can decide how many illustrations to include on each card according to the length of time you envisage each game taking. If you have plenty of help, you could also colour the pictures to add interest. The cards will need to be laminated for regular use.)

Dry-wipe pens or counters to cover the pictures, a set of pictures for the bingo caller, a tray of small prizes such as sweets, fruit, pencils, bath foam.

What to do

1. Place the bingo caller's set of pictures into a container.

2. Give each participant a bingo card and a dry-wipe pen or set of counters.

3. The bingo caller takes one picture at a time out of the container, naming the object for the players and holding it up for them to see.

4. If a player has the named object on their card, they cover it with a counter or draw a line through it with the dry-wipe pen. Make sure that players with sight or co-ordination problems have help in completing their cards.

This continues until a player has one line of their bingo card covered or crossed out.

5. That player chooses a prize.

6. You can continue with another one or two players receiving a prize for completing a line and then play on until someone achieves a full house, with all their pictures covered.

7. When the game is completed, the counters are removed or the cards are wiped clean.

8. The players swap cards and a new game begins.

Figure 3

FEELING GOOD (AN EXERCISE FOR THE LESS MOBILE)

1; W/Ch; ! – noise

Owing to the level of supervision they require, people with learning disabilities are frequently ferried from door to door by taxi and therefore their opportunities for exercise are limited. Many are also 'exercise shy'.

Club nights specifically programmed with exercise or sport in the title can frighten off potential participants. A way round this is to call matters of health and fitness 'Feeling good'.

Have someone to whom the group relates well to talk briefly about the need to keep fit – i.e. covering the following points.

- Exercise:

    o helps our blood move around our bodies which helps keep us warm and heals injuries

    o stops us from getting stiff

    o builds up our muscles

    o shapes us into a fit body on which we can wear smart clothes

    o helps to keep us happy.

- A healthy diet:

    o when we eat too much our bodies become heavy and uncomfortable to carry round

    o keeps our skin clear and free from spots

    o gives us more energy

    o should include water, which helps to keep us feeling well.

Sessions need to be fun otherwise people will be put off. A movement leader should demonstrate each exercise in order to encourage participants. To add to the enjoyment they could be dressed in a comic way, e.g. as Superman or a ballerina.

As a safety precaution, a warming-up period of at least five minutes is essential before beginning more vigorous exercise. Warm ups can include stamping feet, clapping hands, raising knees, waving arms (even chair-bound participants can join in this kind of warm-up). Any music will be with a strong, background beat will be a useful addition.

Following on from the warm-up, the exercises can progress to more vigorous activity up to the level of each individual's comfort. Some participants may be unaware of their limits, so due care needs to be taken in order to avoid injury. Pay particular attention to those participants suffering from asthma, and avoid twisting movements to avoid injury.

A sample session might go as follows:

1. Stretching:

    •   Lower head to each shoulder in turn, then forward and gently backward.

    •   Slide hand down outside of leg as far as it will reach, then repeat for other leg.

    •   Stretch arms in front and bow head slowly.

    •   Seated: stretch out leg in front and point toes. Circle foot. Repeat with other leg.

    •   Circle arms, one at a time.

2. Progress to:

    •   jogging on the spot

    •   steps to side and back

    •   shake limbs

3. For the more active:

- star jumps

- skipping

- fun relay races with dressing up, beanbags on heads, or a simple obstacle course.

Movement to a story

This is an ideal way to introduce exercise to participants who do not relish the idea of sporty activity. It is fun and engaging, and encourages everyone to join in.

The participants stand or sit in a well-spaced semi-circle, so that they can all see the movement leader. It is advisable to run through all the required movements before reading the story. A narrator who has a loud voice is an advantage, or you can use a microphone.

An example of a story is given below. The idea is that movements, (shown in brackets,) are copied as the narrator reads.

Swimming with the animals

It was Jamie James' birthday and, as a special treat, his mother was taking him for a trip to the zoo. Jamie paced from one foot to the other impatiently (*raise and lower each foot in turn*) as they waited in the queue to buy their entrance tickets.

At least he could look over the wall and wave (*wave*) to the animals inside the zoo. He especially liked to watch the sea-lions in their cool, blue pond. Like most boys, he loved to play in water, especially on a hot day like this.

Once inside the zoo, Jamie's mother complained that she was tired after so much standing and they would have to go and have a cup of tea before looking at the animals. Jamie was very disappointed (*frown*), but at least he was able to have a cooling ice-cream. As the lion roared (*large open mouth*), Jamie licked (*lick*) and waved (*wave*) to the monkeys in their enclosure, wishing he could clamber about with them.

Just then a large frog hopped (*jump*) by on its way to a muddy, little pond.

'Look at the mess you are in,' said Jamie's mother. 'I will go and fetch a napkin to wipe your mouth.'

Jamie did not like the idea of his mum scrubbing at his mouth, but the hopping frog (*jump*) had given him an idea. He could wash his mouth in the cool, blue pool he had seen earlier. While his mum's back was turned, Jamie crept off down one of the many pathways.

Knowing it would not be safe to swim (*swimming movement with arms*) alone, Jamie decided to see who might like to go with him. The elephant looked big and strong with large stomping feet (*stamp feet*).

'Would you like to come and swim with me?' Jamie asked politely, but the elephant waved his trunk (*shake head*) and trumpeted "Nooooo". Jamie was secretly relieved, as the elephant was very large and might have taken up all the space in the pool!

Next he saw a cheetah. 'I know you are brilliant at running', said Jamie (*running motion*) 'but are you good at swimming as well?' (*swimming movement*).

'I most surely am,' replied the cheetah 'and my friend, horse, (*high-rise knee trot*) likes to swim too, so I'll go and fetch him'. So saying, he ran off (*run on spot*).

'Hmm', though Jamie 'maybe a horse (*high-rise knee trot*) will take up too much room as well. I think a hedgehog would be a better size, (*close hand into fist*) I'll ask him.'

However, when Jamie asked the hedgehog, it was so shy that it immediately curled up into a tight ball (*bring up legs to chest and curl up*) and would not speak. As Jamie was about to move on, he was surprised by a very excited kangaroo who was jumping and boxing the air at the same time (*depending on mobility, participants jump and/or box the air*).

'Can I come swimming (*swimming motion*) with you?' the kangaroo squealed. 'As long as you don't box me (*box the air*),' Jamie answered. The kangaroo jumped excitedly up and down (*jump*) and followed Jamie, boxing the air (*box air*) happily as it went.

Just at that moment, there was a loud clip-clop (*high-rise knee trot*) as horse trotted up with cheetah. 'By the way,' said cheetah, 'Parrot (*flap arms like wings*) has flown in to join us. He keeps squawking "Fancy a swim? Fancy a swim?"' (*swimming movement*). That pool was going to get a bit crowded at this rate! 'I'd better head to the pool now,' thought Jamie 'before anything else wants to join us.'

As the group walked along, they were met by a penguin coming from the opposite direction (*flap, waddle and clap*). Jamie asked the penguin for directions to the pool and it pointed (*point*) along a path and beckoned (*beckon*) Jamie to follow. The little group followed the penguin (*flap, waddle and clap*). Cheetah ran (*running motion*) up and down to check that everyone was going in the right direction. Horse trotted (*high rise knee trot*) behind Jamie, kangaroo jumped and boxed (*jump and/or box air*) and parrot flew (*flap arms*).

They were just about to dive into the pool when a hand grabbed Jamie's arm. 'Oh no you don't' said his mum. "If you want to go swimming (*swimming movement*), 'I will take you to the safe sports-centre pool tomorrow. Now, let me clean that ice-cream off your face!'

Activity

You could continue the Feeling good session with the activity below.

Equipment

a pile of magazines (containing pictures of food supermarket type are the best)

scissors

glue

3 large sheets paper/card

individually entitled: Anytime Foods

Everyday Foods

Occasional Foods.

What to do

1. Participants cut the food pictures from the magazines and stick them on to the appropriate sheet of paper.

2. These are then exhibited as a wall display.

3. If necessary, guide the participants by saying the following:

    *   Fresh fruit and vegetables would fit into the Any time Foods as the best source of between-meal snacks.

    *   Everyday Foods are what should be in a balanced diet, including meat, fish and dairy products. Portion size should be emphasized as being important.

    *   Occasional Foods are those that are liable to make us overweight and unhealthy, but can be eaten as treats, e.g. cakes, sweets, chips, ice-cream.

4. Try finishing an exercise session with a healthy snack and refreshing drink. For example:

    •   make smoothies from liquidized fruit and vegetables

    •   chop up a fruit salad for everyone

    •   have a healthy sandwich competition.

SPECIAL OCCASIONS

A special occasion event will only take place two or three times a year. Although it may involve considerable preparation time, the pleasure and satisfaction for all those involved is well worth the effort. The event may involve making special equipment, but this can be re-used in subsequent events over and over again. You may decide to invite another club to join you for an event and make it an even bigger occasion!

BET A CHALLENGE!

> L3; W/Ch; V

This event is a real favourite with our group. It works best with a larger audience, so we invite another group to join us for the evening.

Although it does involve a considerable amount of preparation initially, once you have made the resources for it they can be laminated and used again and again. We have detailed some of the ideas that we use, but you can introduce your own challenges as well.

When the 'challenge' involves eating do be aware of any issues relating to food ingestion that the participants might have, and also check with the staff of the visiting group about their members.

Resources

You will need to make a fan (three separate pieces of card joined together) of three colours (red, yellow and blue) held together by a loop of string, large enough to go over an adult's wrist, for every adult attending.

You will also need three sets of large cards of each colour for members of the panel, as well as a means of distinguishing the contestants. This could be large coloured badges or coloured cards of red, yellow and blue with a loop of string to place over their heads and be worn as a necklace. A big, bright banner with the words 'BET A CHALLENGE' adds to the excitement of the evening.

We place a large tin of assorted sweets on a table at the front of our hall. This is where the panellists sit and if they correctly predict the winner of a challenge, they can take a sweet. There is also a basket of small non-food prizes such as notelets, pencils and soaps.

You will also need the resources for each challenge that you include; and these are detailed in the relevant activity.

How to play

1. For each activity, new panellists are chosen and three volunteers from the audience are selected to take on the challenge. In this way, we hope that the majority of the people attending will have the opportunity to actively participate. For those who don't wish to be so actively involved, there is still the fun of trying to choose the winner.

2. At the start of each activity, the challenge is explained to the audience and three volunteers are chosen to participate. They each wear one of the colours.

3. Three panellists are also selected to come and sit at the front table, facing the audience.

4. The members of the audience are then asked to bet on which contestant they think will win the challenge by holding up the matching coloured card on their fans.

5. The panellists do the same, helped by audience suggestions.

The activity commences and continues until a winner is declared. The panellists who have correctly predicted the winner can take a sweet and the winning contestant also receives a prize.

Ideas for challenges

Strong arm
The three contestants are issued with identical cans of, for example, baked beans. On the command 'Go', they must hold the cans out directly in front of them with straight arms. The winner is the player who can maintain this position for the longest time.

Balancing act
On the command 'Go', the contestants must stand on one leg, without holding on to anything for support. The winner is the player who can maintain this position for the longest time.

Balloon race

For this challenge you will need three round blown-up balloons and a newspaper folded flat and sellotaped to make a fan. (You could use scrunched up tissue paper, if you think some of the members are frightened of balloons.) The three contestants start at one end of the hall and use their fans to waft their balloons or tissue paper balls to the other end and the finishing line. They should not use their fans to hit the balloons.

Black tongue

You will need a special sweet from a joke shop for this activity or you could try some liquorice sweets to find one that will leave a black colour on the tongue. You need to move around the audience during a previous activity and ask for three volunteers who would like a sweet. Two of the sweets will be normal boiled sweets but the third should leave colouring on the tongue. When the volunteers have eaten their sweets, they stand at the front of the hall facing the audience, mouths tightly closed. The audience bets on which contestant has the black tongue.

Bullseye

You will need three, tiger-rocket balloons (long balloons inflated by a tube that makes a noise when released, available from toy or party shops) and a bulls-eye target on a card or plastic sheet. The bulls-eye is placed in the centre of the room and the contestants stand at three corners of the room. Three helpers are required to hold the balloons until the game commences. On the command 'Go', the contestants each take hold of an inflated balloon, they point their balloons towards the bulls-eye target and release them. The winner is the player whose balloon lands nearest the target. You can use a length of string to measure the distance if the winner is not obvious.

Wet sponges

! – Beware of playing too near electrical appliances.

For this challenge you will need three buckets with a different coloured label on each and a couple of bath sponges cut into small pieces. You will also need a shower cap, a bin bag with arm and head holes cut out and a plastic sheet. Explain to the audience that you have three buckets. Two of them contain dry sponges, but in the third bucket, the sponges are wet. Ask for a volunteer to sit on a chair at the front and have the sponges thrown at them. The volunteer wears the shower cap and bin bag and has the plastic sheet draped around them and held by two helpers to form a protective booth. The audience and panellists then bet on which coloured bucket contains the wet sponges. You gently throw the contents of each bucket, in turn, at the volunteer.

Football parcels

You will need three plastic balls (the size of a football), wrapping paper and sellotape in a dispenser for each player in this challenge. On the command 'Go', the contestants have to wrap the balls in the paper, making sure that no section of the ball is visible, and secure it with the sellotape. The winner is the first player to completely cover their ball.

Marshmallow mouth

You will need a large tub of marshmallows for this challenge, three plastic bowls and paper towels. This is a hugely popular event, but take care whom you choose to participate as the object of the activity is to see which contestant can hold the most marshmallows in their mouth. They stand in a line at the front and you walk down the line putting a marshmallow into each of the player's hands in turn, until they indicate that they have had enough. They can then spit the marshmallows into the plastic bowls and use the paper towels to wipe their mouths. It is advisable to wear a disposable glove for health and safety reasons. You can add to the hilarity of this game by asking the contestants to say 'Thistles' from time to time (but stand well back).

Whoopee cushion

You will need three chairs, three seat covers and a whoopee cushion. Choose three contestants and give them their colours. Ask them to leave the room and place the blown-up whoopee cushion on one of the chairs. Cover all the seats. Ask the audience and panellists to vote on which person will sit on the chair with the whoopee cushion. Invite the contestants back into the room and ask them, one at a time, to choose a chair to sit on. Whatever colour the 'flatulant' player is wearing, wins!

PANCAKE PARTY ('PANCAKES WITHOUT PANIC')

Pre-advertising this event will allow carers to make adjustments to participants' dietary needs – they may need to eat less before the event).

> L2; W/Ch; ! – hot equipment

You will need approximately an hour and a half to make and eat the pancakes.

Equipment

A two-ring cooker,

2 medium non-stick frying pans,

2 pan spatulas,

2 heat-resistant mats to stand the hot pans on,

clean gardening gloves for the participants to wear whilst tossing their pancakes (these make ideal hand protection),

a jug,

clean sheet and small rubber-backed mat for participants to stand on,

plates and spoons,

pancake mixture in plastic bottle, ready to pour into jug: for 40 persons you will need – 600g flour; 1,500 ml water; 9 tablespoons dried milk powder; 6 eggs,

cooking oil,

lemon juice, and caster sugar,

tables for the cooker, heat-resistant mats and sugar and lemon station.

The room layout is a very important safety feature in this event (See Figure 4). No one must stand in front of the cooker or cross the 'tossing' path. You can use a wall of chairs to mark the boundary. This also allows a good view of the proceedings so that people will not be jostling for positions to watch the tossing.

You will need the following helpers:

- a cook (someone experienced, calm and confident)

- two helpers to marshal the waiting participants and ensure that they are wearing the protective gloves when it is their turn to toss the pancake

- a helper to organize the tossing (someone calm and confident)

- one or two helpers to place the plates by the heat-resistant mats and to distribute sugar and lemon once the pancakes are ready to eat.

What to do

1. The cook prepares thin pancakes, fully cooked on both sides, for the participants.

2. Participants can stand at the side of the cooker, one at a time and wearing gloves, to watch their pancake being cooked.

3. Once the pancake is ready, the pan is placed on a heat-resistant mat by the cook.

4. The helper in charge of tossing ensures that the participant is holding the pan securely and safely and is in the correct position on the mat by the clean sheet.

5. The helper guides the participant to tilt the outside edge of the pan slightly downwards and allow the pancake to slide towards the rim.

6. On the count of three, the pancake is tossed with a quick upwards movement of the hands.

7. If the pancake fails to return to the pan, but lands on the clean sheet, it can be carefully lifted with a spatula and transferred to a plate to be eaten.

8. The successful pancake tosser returns the pan to a heat-resistant mat where a helper transfers the pancake onto a plate.

9. The participant removes the gloves and takes their plate to the finishing table for lemon, sugar and a spoon.

In case of burns

Participants should be well protected with sleeves rolled down and wearing gloves. Also have a replacement cook on standby in case of minor accidents. If the cook or a helper does burn a finger, have a bucket of cold water nearby in which to plunge the burnt area. The scalded area then needs to be held under cold, running water for at least ten minutes.

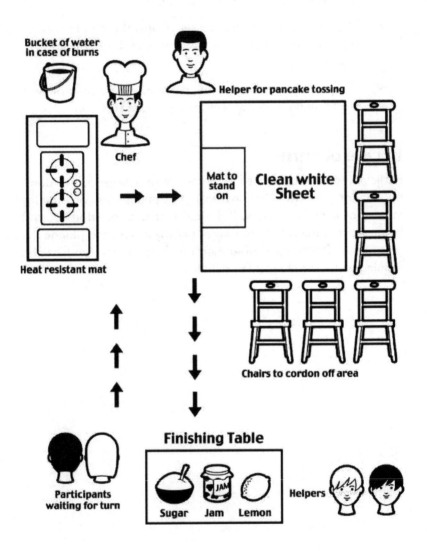

Figure 4

VALENTINE'S DAY QUIZ

L2; W/Ch; V

Equipment

You will need two large, card hearts (one for each team) and a box of smaller hearts, blu-tac, three-colour card fans (red, yellow and blue) for each player, (see Bet a Challenge on page 82), a set of questions (see below).

What to do

1. Each question has a multiple-choice answer denoted by the colours. The players are put into two teams 'Hugs' and 'Kisses'.

2. The participants in each team take turns to come out to the front and hold the colour fan to display the colour of their chosen answer.

3. If they choose the correct answer, they can stick one of the small hearts onto their large heart (the other members of the team can hold up the colours of their chosen answer to help their team mate decide).

4. At the end of the quiz, the small hearts are counted and the team with the most is the winner.

Ideas for questions

1. What is Valentine's Day?

   (R) A time for eating pancakes

   (B) When one person tells another person they love them

   (Y) A man called Valentine's birthday

2. In what month is Valentine's Day?

   (Y) January

   (R) February

   (B) December

3. On what date is Valentine's Day?

   (B) 15th

   (Y) 14th

   (R) 25th

4. What is the Valentine's Day special colour?

   (R) Red

   (B) Blue

   (Y) Yellow

5. What is love?

   (R) A song

   (Y) Your favourite dinner

   (B) A nice feeling you have for someone else

6. What is romantic love?

   (Y) Love for your family

   (B) Special feelings for a girlfriend or boyfriend

   (R) That happy feeling you have when you eat a bar of chocolate

7. Romeo was famous for being in love. What was his girlfriend called?

   (B) Victoria

   (R) Juliet

   (Y) Valentine

8. Which of these is a clue that a couple are in love?

   (R) Holding hands

   (Y) Buying mobile phones

   (B) Stamping on each other's toes

9. If you asked someone to be your Valentine, would it be because:

   (Y) They grew nice roses

   (B) You loved them

   (R) They made a great partner for playing computer games

10. Who is Popeye's girlfriend?

    (R) Tomato Ketchup

    (Y) Olive Oil

    (B) Salad Cream

11. Who would Minnie Mouse have for a boyfriend?

    (B) Peter Rabbit

    (R) Bugs Bunny

    (Y) Mickey Mouse

12. What flowers are usually given on Valentine's Day?

    (Y) Carnations

    (R) Daffodils

    (B) Roses

13. Which symbol stands for a kiss? (Draw onto a large card to hold up)

    (R) ?

    (Y) X

    (B) +

14. What do people stand under at Christmas when they want a kiss?

    (Y) Holly

    (B) Mistletoe

    (R) Umbrella

15. What was the name of Superman's girlfriend?

    (B) Lois Lane

    (R) Mary Jane

    (Y) (name a female helper)

16. What light is meant to make a room look romantic?

    (R) Sunlight

    (Y) Candlelight

    (B) Torchlight

17. How are Eskimos supposed to kiss?

    (Y) Rub noses

    (B) Pat bottoms

    (R) Suck each other's thumbs

18. If your boyfriend asked to take you on a date, would he:

    (B) Sit you down on a large fruit

    (R) Write your name on a calendar

    (Y) Take you somewhere nice

19. Who was Adam in the Bible's lady friend?

    (R) Mary

    (Y) Eve

    (B) Elizabeth

20. What is an engagement?

    (Y) When two people promise to marry each other

    (B) When someone else is on the telephone

    (R) A new way to kiss

21. Where do married people wear their rings?

   (B) In their noses

   (R) Around their necks

   (Y) On their fingers

22. Who is the Queen married to?

   (R) King Cole

   (Y) Popeye

   (B) Prince Philip

23. What is a honeymoon?

   (Y) A holiday a couple share after they are married

   (B) A moon-shaped biscuit made with honey

   (R) When bees fall in love

24. What is a wedding anniversary?

   (B) A book of wedding photos

   (R) A time each year when a wedding is remembered

   (Y) Someone who hates weddings

25. What part of the body is used as a Valentine symbol?

   (R) Heart

   (B) Nose

   (Y) Teeth

26. Which pantomime has a romantic story?

   (B) Puss in Boots

   (Y) Jack and the Beanstalk

   (R) Beauty and the Beast

27. Finish the poem: Roses are red, Violets are:

   (R) Green

   (B) Blue

   (Y) Tartan

28. Who was Cleopatra's Lover?

   (Y) Winston

   (R) Marc Anthony

   (B) Benjamin

29. Who did Prince Charming marry?

   (Y) An ugly sister

   (R) The wicked step-mother

   (B) Cinderella

30. Which two people at your club are married? (club orga-
   nizers should use staff names for incorrect answers.)

   (R)

   (Y)

   (B)

EASTER BONNET PARADE

L3; W/Ch

Equipment

Using the bonnet templates (in Figure 5), cut out sufficient bonnets for your members each to make one. You will also need tissue paper discs for the flowers, egg shapes of coloured foil, chicks and rabbits, florist's or material-ribbon scissors, glue, staplers to attach the ribbon.

What to do

1. Each member of the group is invited to make a bonnet, with plenty of help available if required.

2. At the end of the evening, the chairs are placed in a circle and all the participants, two or three at a time, can wear their bonnets and parade around the inside of the circle to applause from the seated audience. (N.B. Bonnets may be fragile until the glue is completely dried.)

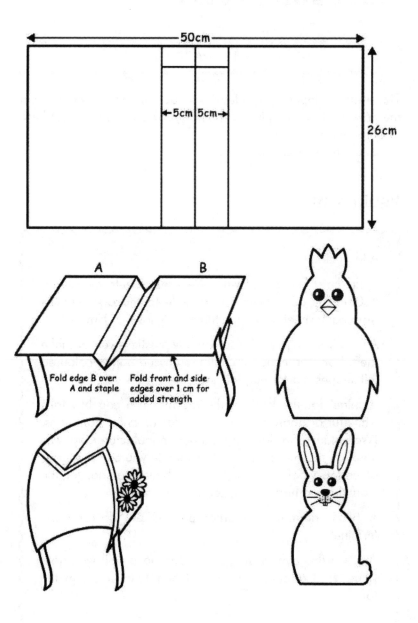

Figure 5

RIGHT ROYAL EVENT

L3; W/Ch

This event is ideal to coincide with an actual royal event that is in the news such as a jubilee, centenary, royal wedding, royal birth or coronation.

It covers two sessions.

Equipment

A long cloak

Gold card for the crowns. We used sheets measuring 510mm by 635mm and were able to make six crowns from each sheet, using the template shown in Figure 6.

A selection of 'jewels'. You can buy plastic jewels or make them from scrunched up coloured tissue paper, coloured felt shapes, Easter egg foil, sweet wrappers, etc.

'Ermine' for the base of the crowns. You can buy fake white fur or approach local manufacturers for donations. (We obtained wadding from a bed manufacturer that was ideal.) If these options aren't available you can use strips of cotton wool. You might also obtain material for the cloak from a furniture maker or fabric shop.

A black permanent marker pen to put dots on the 'ermine'.

An orb: this can be made by covering a ball with gold paper and adding sequins and a golden cross on the top.

A sceptre: this can be made by spraying tubing with gold spray paint and gluing on sequins.

A throne: this can be as elaborate or simple as you choose. You can spray card cut-outs with gold paint to place over the chair or just drape it with some suitable material.

A digital camera and printing facility.

Session one

1. All the members make a crown, with plenty of help available if required.

2. Use UHU solvent-free glue to make sure the 'jewels' and 'ermine' are stuck on adequately.

3. Measure each person's crown around their heads, write their names inside and fasten with a stapler.

Session two

1. Each participant in turn wears their crown and the cloak.

2. They are announced to the assembled company as 'His/Her Majesty King/Queen _____.'

3. They are led to the throne and handed the orb and sceptre.

4. Each participant is applauded by the audience and has their photograph taken.

5. Print out the photographs and give them to the participants.

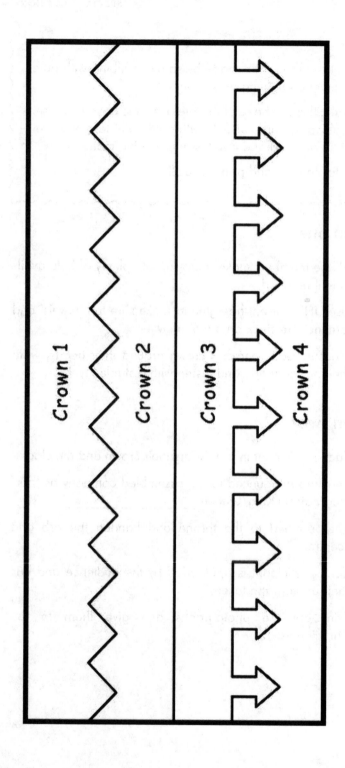

Crown 1

Crown 2

Crown 3

Crown 4

Figure 6

INDOOR FETE

L3; W/Ch

Fetes are always very popular and organizing an indoor event ensures that it will not be marred by poor weather.

Tables are placed around the venue with various attractions. It is also a good idea to include a free raffle. Canvass local businesses and patrons for donations and use funds to buy small prizes so that all the games are free.

In addition to having helpers on each stall, try and find a few volunteers to encourage your club members to join in and play the games.

Ideas for stalls

Treasure map

A large island can be drawn onto a grid of squares. On the underside, an 'X' marks the position of buried treasure (if you think players may turn the map over to cheat, you can write down the whereabouts of the treasure and place in a sealed envelope). The participants are invited to choose a square on the grid where they think the treasure is buried. Their names are written onto that square (only one name allowed per square). The winner is the person nearest to the treasure.

Hunt the flea on the cat

Prepare a large drawing of a cat. This can be covered in fake fur if you have some available. Mark a place on the underside to denote the position of the flea. Invite participants to guess the flea's whereabouts and use flag pins with their names on to show their guesses. The winner is the person nearest to the flea.

Name the teddy/doll/soft toy

Display the prize and invite participants to think of a suitable name. Write this name and the player's name on a piece of paper. At the end of the event, put all the names into a box, give them a good shake and pick one out. This will be the winning name. If you think your players will have difficulties thinking of names, you can make a chart with a selection of names printed on and players can choose one to write their name alongside. You can either have a pre-selected winning name for the teddy/doll/soft toy, or you can put all the names into a box and pick one out.

Pin the tail on the mouse

Enlarge the template in Figure 7 to A3 size for your mouse. You will also need a tail of wool or a shoe-lace. The participants wear a blind-fold and you gently turn them round once and guide them to the 'mouse'. They are given the tail and they indicate where they think it should be positioned. You attach the tail to the 'mouse' with blu-tac and remove their blind-fold. Use initials to mark each player's guess. The winner is the player whose tail is nearest to the correct position.

Sand game

Push lolly sticks up to halfway into a sand tray. Some of the lolly sticks have 'winner' written onto their concealed halves. If a player picks out a winning lolly stick they receive a small prize.

Snap cards

Use a set of picture snap cards. Place 15–20 of the cards face down on the table. Each player is given one of the remaining matching cards. They can turn over five cards on the table to see if they can find a match for their card. If they find a match, they receive a small prize.

Target practice

Place six or seven medium-sized plastic flower pots on the floor in two rows. The participants stand some distance from their targets (you can alter this distance according to their capabilities). They have three bean-bags to throw and must get one into a flower-pot to win a prize.

Guess the contents

Several identical jars or tubs with lids are each filled with a different item such as pebbles, drawing pins, split peas and oat flakes. Each jar is labelled with a different letter. Samples of the items inside the jars are displayed on a table. The players shake the jars to try and guess what's inside each one. They place each jar alongside the item they think it contains. If they have guessed correctly they win a prize.

Figure 7

FANCY-DRESS SPONSORED WALK

L3; W/Ch; ! – be aware of mobility problems and ensure that
there are sufficient helpers to allow everyone to have a go

This event is a good photo opportunity for the local press to publicize your organization.

This is an ideal way to raise sponsorship money, but you will need to remind the participants about doing so several weeks ahead of the event. They can wear any fancy dress they like and there will be a prize each for the best male and female outfit. You will find an example of a sponsor form in Figure 8.

The preparations cover two sessions.

Session prior to the event

During the session prior to the event help participants to make flag markers with A4 paper and small garden canes. They can decorate their markers with cut-out illustrations from magazines or coloured paper shapes, or use templates to draw round and cut out on coloured paper. These flags are used to mark the circuit of the walk.

Design a one-way circuit either indoors or outside, or even a combination of both. Make sure that the toilet access is left free and include a 'rest and refreshment station'. The circuit can be marked with chairs and the flags from the previous session.

To put at the start of the circuit you will need a large board showing all the participants' names alongside a tally chart of the laps they have completed and two helpers to fill in the results.

Session when event takes place

1. Make sure that everyone who needs assistance to complete the circuit has a designated helper, and be mindful of those participants who may tire quickly and need frequent rests.

SPONSORSHIP FORM (for name of club, event and date)

We the undersigned pledge to sponsor (name) _____

for the sponsored _____ on (date)_____

Name	Address	Amount per lap	Total amount due	Paid

Thank you for your support

For further information contact _____ on _____

Figure 8

2. Half-way through the event stop the proceedings so that everyone has a drink and a rest.

3. Give each participant a certificate recording their name and the number of laps they have completed. It is best to issue these on the night to ensure that the correct amount of sponsor money is then collected.

Once all the sponsor money has been collected

Once this has happened we hold an award ceremony. You can buy inexpensive plastic medals on ribbons for all the participants and we award a prize each for:

- the participant who completed the most laps

- the participant who made the most effort and

- the participant who collected the most sponsor money.

MAKE YOUR OWN HARVEST SUPPER

L3; W/Ch; M; ! – sharp knives

Equipment

A dish containing oasis (attached with florist's anchorage tape) for each table and a selection of stiff-stemmed flowers and greenery (a few carnations and stalks of greenery will suffice).

Table coverings – this can depend on your budget. You can either provide tablecloths for each table, use a roll of suitable paper or even use a row of paper napkins down the centre of each table.

Plates, knives and forks.

For each person provide: one bread roll, a slice of ham, 50g of cheese, and half a tomato.

You will also need 2 iceberg lettuces and 2 cucumbers per 20 people and a tub of spreadable butter.

In addition to these you can provide optional extras such as salad cream, pickled onions, pickle, coleslaw and chopped sweet yellow peppers.

What to do

1. On the evening of the event, divide the participants into groups with various tasks, each group having a helper or two to supervise. Those handling food, crockery or cutlery will need to wash their hands, so it may be advisable to have a couple of bowls of warm water, soap and towels ready on a table. Arrange the groups at tables spread around the room.

2. One group will lay the tables, another will make the flower arrangements, a third group can wash and chop the salad ingredients and grate the cheese, a fourth group can butter the rolls and a fifth group can put the items onto plates.

3. When the tables are set with the filled plates and accompaniments, everyone is invited to sit down and eat.

AWARDS CEREMONY

L3; W/Ch

Once a year we hold an awards ceremony, preceded by some form of entertainment. This might be a disco or a musical evening where a performer, such as a keyboard player, is invited in to entertain the audience.

If you are able to, organize a visit by a local dignitary, e.g. the mayor or carnival queen, to hand out the awards. Club members particularly like to see people dressed in their official regalia.

The main award that we give is an achievement cup. This could be awarded for a variety of reasons such as:

- for achieving greater independence of life-style

- for being involved in voluntary work

- for always looking after a special friend

- for making speeches on behalf of the club and others

- for showing bravery in the face of illness

- for achieving a slimming goal

- for always being ready to lend a hand

- for overcoming/remaining cheerful in the face of difficulties.

You can also use the occasion to hand out other awards for a recently held event such as a sponsored walk, a talent competition or art competition.

Invite the local press to photograph the ceremony and include a short paragraph in the paper.

DRAMA AND DANCE

Drama, music and dance can provide great enjoyment for people with learning disabilities. Sounds, rhythms and beats are often easily accessible and can be a major source of entertainment for people who struggle with language and comprehension – focusing on a particular beat can have a very liberating effect. Since drama, music and dance are languages of their own, these can act as a special means of expression for those people unable to communicate effectively in spoken language. Music and dance also provide valuable opportunities to encourage physical exercise for people who may seldom be very active otherwise – and in an enjoyable way that doesn't appear too difficult.

Drama offers valuable opportunities to express ideas and emotions without the constraints of language. Participants can develop imaginative skills and enjoy watching each other perform. Moreover, drama encourages social interaction in a stimulating and fun way that motivates people to join in. However, whilst some can easily slip into acting, be aware that for others the lines between make-believe and reality can become blurred and confusing. Pretend fights and quarrels can be distressing, so caution and care is needed.

When introducing drama to your group for the first time, try something small-scale such as dressing up in different hats to stand in character. Mime making a drink or something to eat, then progress to acting out a familiar event or story. A visit to a pantomime provides a good follow-up opportunity. Such small-scale activities may be the limit of some of your members.

The more adventurous and capable members of your group will enjoy the opportunity to improvise their own plays and perform them to the group. This still needs supervision and direction to make sure the story-line is coherent and the performance is not overly long.

TALENT SHOW

```
L2; W/Ch
```

It is advisable to give several weeks' notice to this event, and to explain that everyone is good at something and it is better to celebrate this, rather than focus on winners.

Contact parents and carers, urging them to encourage an entry and make suitable suggestions for participants.

You may like to use the following list of categories, or, if you think that the range is too wide, you can separate the items into individual events of art, music or drama.

- *Drama*: this category could include:

   o reciting poetry, telling a joke, giving a speech, acting a sketch

- *Movement*: this category could include:

   o dance, circus act, sports display

- *Music*: this category could include:

   o singing, playing an instrument

- *Art*: this category could include:

   o painting, ceramics, photography, textiles such as needlework or printing on fabric, drawing, computer-generated picture, any other crafts

- *Hobby*: talk about and/or demonstrate a hobby.

- *Best smile*: everyone can demonstrate this talent, so it is worth including this category. Many of us are deeply moved by a single smile.

Judges

Choose a panel of judges (three is the most workable) well in advance of the event, in order to include suitable people. While experts in a particular field may be appealing, you do need to ensure that the judges you enlist have a sympathy and understanding of people with learning disabilities. If it is possible, try to include a figurehead, such as the mayor, as the presence of a local celebrity would be much appreciated by the participants – and it could also provide the opportunity for a photo in the press and thus raise the profile of your group locally.

Prizes

Prepare certificates or token prizes for all the entrants as a reward for their effort and participation. Certificates can be cheaply and easily produced on a computer, naming the entrant and praising them for entering the competition.

Presentation cups can be bought for the winners, but if this option is too expensive, other suitable prizes could be: mugs, drinking glasses, photo frames, pens, rosettes and medals. These may be found in school catalogues or the party section at your local supermarket.

Room preparation

Try and set the scene using any props available to make the session more special. A stage or platform adds a touch of class, though you will have to take care where steps or a height difference are concerned. Curtains and drapes, along with a smart, judges' table will all help to create the desired ambience, and you will need to arrange the spectators' chairs so that everyone has a good view of the proceedings.

Arrange for a standing microphone, if possible, and ensure that any extraneous objects are removed from the performance area so as not to spoil photographs of the participants.

Scoring

Scoring can be carried out through discussion amongst the judges or by using a points system. Each judge could have a list of entrants and award competitors a score out of ten. An alternative method is for judges to hold up score cards and a helper fills in a chart.

For art exhibits, a period is required during which the judges can view each item. Items should be clearly marked with the entrant's name or given a number. Encouraging comments such as: 'Lovely use of colour', 'This drawing made me feel happy', 'Nice neat stitching' attached to the exhibits on post-it notes are greatly appreciated by the entrants.

At the end of the competition, during the refreshment time, the individual scores are worked out to identify the winners of each category. These are then announced and prizes distributed at the end of refreshment time.

COUNTRY DANCE

L3; V; ! – arrange for additional helpers to partner anyone who might have some mobility problems and ensure adequate space is left between participants

For many years, our club has enjoyed barn/country dancing. Our kindly, local caller chooses dances with simple movements and is very patient. You could approach barn/country or line dancing clubs or organizations in your area to see if anyone would be willing to come in and call for your club members. However, it is wise to investigate your choice very thoroughly before the event as we have experienced a disastrous evening when the routines were overly complicated for members to perform.

Although this is not an activity for wheelchair users or members with very poor mobility, these members can still enjoy the spectacle and listen to the music. Some dancers will need to be partnered with a helper if they have mobility problems or are likely to find the instructions confusing. It is, therefore, a useful exercise to invite parents/carers to attend the session and join in the activity.

Make known in advance that suitable footwear and clothing will be required in order to avoid ankle injuries and overheating, and you will need to have a constant supply of drinks available as dancing is hot work! Ensure that the drinks table is well away from the dancing area in order to avoid dangerous spillage.

You could, as we have also done, organize and run a dance session yourselves. We combined ours with a 'sausage and mash' supper which was very popular, and members were invited to wear 'western' costume to add to the occasion.

We chose a CD of suitable country and western music with a well-defined beat and worked out a selection of simple dance routines to the songs. Below are some ideas that you could incorporate into your own routines:

1. Members stand in a large, well-spaced circle. To help with finding their partners, you could number them 1 and 2 consecutively around the circle.

2. Everyone holds hands and takes 8 steps in a clock-wise direction, then 8 in an anti-clockwise direction.

3. They take 4 steps towards the centre of the circle, then 4 steps out again, or number 1s do this action first, then number 2s.

4. Everyone points and taps right foot twice then points and taps left foot twice.

5. Everyone claps to the right, claps to the left.

6. Everyone claps under their right knee then claps under their left knee.

7. Each number 1 turns to the number 2 on their left. Number 1 holds the hand of number 2 in the air and walks a circle around their partner. Number 2 holds the hand of number 1 in the air and walks a circle around their partner.

8. Number 1 and 2 hold hands and circle on the spot.

9. Number 1 and 2 hold hands and promenade around the circle side by side.

10. Number 2s stand still and number 1s walk in and out of the circle in a clock-wise direction for eight beats, so they end up with a new partner.

You can build on these simple movements if your participants are more capable. Whatever the level of expertise, you can be assured that your members will appreciate and enjoy a session of music and dancing!

Use of props

To add interest to an 'own version' line dance, a hat or cane can be passed from hand to hand and twirled. Not only does this add to the fun, it is also easier to follow than foot movements. When dancing in a line formation, the dance leader should be at the front of the line to demonstrate directional movements, otherwise 'left' and 'right' can get very muddled.

IMAGINARY OUTING

L1; W/Ch

Equipment

Arrange the seating, bus style, in rows of four chairs with a central aisle. Place a 'driver's seat' at the front. For small groups, you could arrange two rows of chairs facing each other. You will need a copy of the story script below.

What to do

1. Take a little time to explain the difference between make-believe and reality so that no one is disappointed that they are not going on a real ride. You could show an example of a real and a plastic apple by taking a bite from the real apple and pretending to eat the plastic one. Ask your members to pretend they are drinking tea from a mug. They can put in the milk and sugar and stir the tea, before miming the act of drinking.

2. Follow on by issuing an invitation to everyone: 'Who'd like to come on a pretend horse and cart ride with me?'

3. Count up the participants and make sure that you have sufficient places in your 'cart'. Instruct everyone to put on some sturdy boots as you are going for a trip to the country-side and to put on their coats (mime these actions).

4. You can either use the script below or ad-lib your own story-line, changing the names for members of your group. (It is probably advisable to have a narrator and a director

to demonstrate the mimes, as it can be quite tricky trying to keep your place in the text whilst showing the actions.)

'Oh, look, everybody, the horse and cart have arrived. Follow me up the path, oops! I've stepped in a puddle. You will have to jump over the puddle or walk round it (*jump over imaginary puddle*). Here we are at the back of the cart – up the steps to climb inside. (*step up in between chairs and find a seat for everyone*). I see you have sat in the front seat, so you will be driving the horse in a minute – catch hold of the reins. (*The director stands behind the driver facing the passengers*).

Last one in close the door. All sitting comfortably? Hold tight as the track is a bit bumpy until we meet the road. Off you go driver, giddy-up horse. Oh it is a bit bumpy. (*encourage everyone to bounce and sway in their seats*).

Watch out for the low tree branch (*duck down*), round the corner (*lean to one side*) and through the farm-yard. Pooh! What a pong! (*hold nose*). Look – pigs (*point right*), that's where the smell is coming from. The gateway's narrow, will we get through?

Everyone hold in your arms (*look worried and hold arms tightly to sides*). Safely through and now we're on a smooth road (*sway gently*).

What pretty flowers in the hedgerow (*point down to the left*). They smell better than the farm-yard. Ooh! Did you see that bird fly from the hedge? There it goes, overhead (*trace with your finger*).

The hill is a bit steep (*sway slower*). Give that horse lots of encouragement everyone (*all shout "gee up, Dobbin"*). The sun's coming out, I expect he's feeling hot – we are (*fan face with hands*). Take your coat off if you wish (*mime removing coat*) and put on your sun glasses (*mime putting on glasses*).

Look over the brow of the hill (*point*), can you see those cows eating the grass next to the railway track? Here comes a train. Whoosh! (*turn head sharply*).

Look to your right (*point*), we're going past the village school. Wave to the children in the playground (*all wave*). We're nearly there now, just round this sharp corner into the field (*lean*), over the bumpy bits (*bounce on seats*) and stop by the stream. Now, I've a surprise for you – I've brought a picnic. Get down carefully from the cart (*everyone exits cart*) and come and sit on the picnic blanket [if sitting on the floor poses problems for some participants, organize chairs as 'deck chairs']. John, here is a nose-bag for the horse to eat – can you give it to him please (*mime actions*). He might like to have his neck stroked.

Everyone ready for the picnic? Jane, you hand round the sandwiches, Simon take the cakes, Hamid give out the bags of crisps. Who would like a banana or an apple? Alisha, would you offer everyone some fruit. Ben, you must be hungry – you've forgotten to take the skin off your banana! (*all mime actions*).

Hold out your cup if you would like some lemonade. Alison, will go round and pour. Enjoy your meal everyone (*all mime eating and drinking*).

Those clouds look dark over there. Oh, I've just felt a spot of rain and another (*hold out upturned palms*). Better drink up everyone. We had better pack up all our rubbish quickly. Gemma, can you take round the black bag for everyone's empty crisp packets and banana skins, except Ben's that is (*mime actions*). Right everyone – back into the cart as quickly as you can, mind the step as you climb in (*everyone gets back into the cart*). Gee up, driver, let's get going, over the bumpy field and round the corner (*mime actions*). Might as well take off our sunglasses now (*mime taking off sunglasses*) and put our coats back on (*mime putting on coats*).

Hello children (wave) – not many of them waving now, they're all running for shelter.

What's that noise? (*put hands over ears*). It's a low-flying aeroplane. It's raining harder now – time to put up umbrellas I think (*mime putting up and holding umbrellas*). Round the corner (*lean*) and into the farm-yard. Hold your nose! I'm getting pretty wet – how about you? Round the next corner (*lean*). Watch out driver, we are going to hit that huge puddle – oh too late! Now we are drenched (*mime shaking water off hands and body*). Along the bumpy track (*bounce on chairs*). Mind that low hanging branch (*all duck down*). Whoops, there goes Ali's umbrella, left hanging in the tree and, Mary, if you had ducked your hat might still be on your head rather than on the ground!

Look, (*point to the right*) the farm dog has taken a fancy to it and run off with it in her mouth.

Here we are, safely home, and it seems to have stopped raining so you can all put your umbrellas down again (*mime actions*). I'll let you off the cart first Mary, so that you can chase after the dog for your hat (*open door*). Mind the step.

That's the end of our country-side ride – thumbs up if you enjoyed the trip.

When you get off, you can all take a sugar lump or a piece of carrot from my bowl to feed to the horse as a "thank you" (*mime actions*).'

ACT AN ACTION

L1; W/Ch

Equipment

This activity involves the participants in simple mimes. Make a list of various everyday activities that your members might carry out such as:

make a phone call, make a cup of tea, make a sandwich, do the washing up, take a dog for a walk, hang clothes on a washing line, buy and eat an ice-cream, colour in a picture, write and post a letter, take a taxi ride, sweep the floor, wash their hair, clean a pair of shoes.

What to do

1. The group sits in a large circle and the participants take turns, one at a time, to mime one of the activities for the others to guess.

2. Try to match the activity to the participant's acting ability.

3. If the watchers are unable to guess the activity they can ask questions such as:

   • 'Where would you do this?'

   • 'Can you eat this?'

4. Place a time limit on the guessing so that participants don't become bored.

DRUMMING

L1; W/Ch; V; ! – some members may dislike noise and may therefore need to be in another room with a quiet activity

Equipment

The beat and rhythm of drumming can be very stimulating and provide an enjoyable form of expression for people with learning disabilities.

It is possible to hire experts who will run superb drumming sessions and provide a wonderful array of suitable instruments, but this is often an expensive option. However, with a little ingenuity and creativity you can still produce an enjoyable DIY drumming session. It may be possible to borrow drumming equipment from a local school, but if this is not an option look around for suitable alternatives. Some ideas are given below:

- Drums: knees, table tops, up-turned cardboard box, empty ice-cream tub, up-turned waste bin, large empty can (make sure there are no sharp edges), up-turned plastic flower pot, up-turned bucket, block of wood.

- Beaters: hands, chop-sticks, rubber tipped pencils, spoons.

Be aware that hands can get sore and blister after a lot of impact. Some of the beaters, such as spoons, can be very noisy and the flimsy drums may be quickly flattened.

A 'conductor' will be needed to ensure the activity is purposeful and the noise level is controlled.

What to do

1. The participants sit in a large circle with a drum each. You might like to organize the same types of drums sitting together.

2. The conductor stands in the centre of the circle.

3. Before the drumming begins, instruct the participants on the commands that you will be giving with your hands. With one hand you will need to make different and distinct hand movements for 'louder' and 'softer' while with the other you will need to be indicating the rhythm. Both hands raised could mean stop.

4. Begin the session with everyone drumming a regular, even beat, then increase and decrease the volume. The conductor drums first and the participants echo the sound.

5. Once the participants can follow your commands, move on to something a little more adventurous, e.g. a question and response section where drumming accompanies the spoken words. For example, you might drum to each group 'Who are you?' and their response would be, for example, 'We are the bucket drums' or 'We are the tin can drums'. Each participant could take a turn at drumming their name e.g. 'My name is David', 'My name is Alison'.

6. The participants might like to drum questions to each other in the circle.

7. Introduce some rhythm with words of varying syllables, including 'rests' in between.

   Saus-a-ges *rest rest* saus-a-ges *rest rest*

   Chips *rest* chips *rest*

   Ket-chup *rest rest* ket-chup *rest rest*

   Eggs *rest rest rest* eggs *rest rest rest*

8. Divide the participants into four equal groups and give each group one of the above phrases to drum. Start the groups off, one at a time, until all four are drumming their phrases together.

9. You might also like to include some recorded songs and use a CD with popular, well-known titles or marching songs that the participants can accompany.

MIME THE OBJECT

L1; W/Ch; ! – be aware of any
potentially dangerous moves with objects

Equipment

A selection of objects to use as miming aids, e.g. walking stick, card-insert from a large roll of sellotape, bucket, cardboard tube, blanket, piece of rope, tumble-drier outlet tube, large book, cardboard box.

What to do

1. The participants sit in a large circle.

2. Introduce one of the objects and demonstrate how they could use the prop to mime various activities, e.g. if the prop was a walking stick, they could pretend it was a guitar and mime playing it, or they might use it as a hockey stick or a sword. (You may need to warn them about safety as pretending the stick was a javelin, for example, and throwing it would not be a sensible option.)

3. If the object was the card-insert from a roll of sellotape, they might pretend it was a bracelet, a hoopla or a lid on a jar.

4. Place the objects, one at a time, in the centre of the circle and invite the participants to take turns to pick up the prop and perform their mime for the others to guess.

STRIKE A POSE

L1; W/Ch; ! – be aware of any participant who
may be unsteady on their feet

The aim behind this activity is to have fun and for participants to amuse one another with their outlandish poses!

What to do

1. Explain to participants that the object of the activity is to strike and hold a pose for a variety of situations that you will call out to them. It may be a good idea to demonstrate a few such as playing tennis or football, climbing a tree and blowing up a balloon.

2. Explain that they need to exaggerate their movement in order to make their pose more effective.

3. If you think someone's pose is particularly good, encourage the other participants to view it and give the person a round of applause.

4. Some examples of situations are:

   • running

   • skating on ice

   • flying a kite

   • swimming the crawl

   • brushing their teeth

   • putting the star on the top of the Christmas tree

   • playing the piano

   • walking through a haunted house at the fairground

- pushing a heavy boulder up a hill
- looking for a small ear-ring in a leafy forest floor
- washing an elephant's back.

SOUNDS AND NOISES

L2; W/Ch; V; ! – be aware of people pushing and jostling if anyone is unsteady on their feet

ANIMAL FARM

Equipment

Sets of cards (five or six in each set) of animals with distinctive calls (e.g. cows, dogs, cats, ducks, sheep) – enough for each member to have a card.

What to do

1. Explain to members you will be giving each person a card with an animal picture on it. They must look at their animal, but not show it to anyone else. On the command 'Go', they must all mill around in the middle of the room, making their animal noise. The object of the game is to find the other members of their animal set, by recognizing their animal sound.

2. It is a good idea to go through the animals and agree on the sound each one will make before playing.

3. Shuffle the cards well and give them out.

4. When all the players have sorted themselves into the correct sets, you can collect in the cards and play the game again.

LISTENING GAME

Equipment

A recording of familiar sounds, e.g. vacuum cleaner, filling a bath with water, a lawn mower, a kettle boiling, a motor bike, a dog barking, a clock ticking, a toilet flushing, a clock alarm. Try to get 20–30 different sounds.

What to do

1. Divide the participants into two evenly matched teams.

2. Make sure that each team has a scribe to number and write down the answers.

3. Ask the scribe to write down the numbers 1 onwards, before you begin.

4. Place the teams as far apart as possible, then play the sounds recording, one at a time.

5. Repeat each sound before you move on to the next one.

6. Encourage the teams to have a guess, even if they are unsure of the answer. If they do leave a blank, remind the players to go on to the next number for the following sound.

7. When you have played all the sounds, go through them again. After each sound ask alternate teams for their answer.

8. They tick each one correct.

9. At the end, they add up their score to see which team is the winner.

SOUNDS STORY

Equipment

All you need is the inter-active 'sounds' story given below and a helper. However, if you have access to musical instruments such as tambourines or xylophones, the story can be adapted to include these.

What to do

1. Arrange the participants so that they are seated behind tables in a semi-circle.

2. Place some plastic or paper bags on the tables.

3. If you have instruments then place these on the tables and include other sentences in the text such as:

   • The windchimes tinkled in the wind (*shake tambourines*)

   • I heard a clock chime 10 o'clock (*strike a note on the xylophone ten times*)

4. You will need to sit behind a table facing the participants, alongside a helper who will demonstrate the sounds and actions for everyone to copy, as you read the story.

Interactive sounds story

It was late one night and as I was walking home, I was caught in a sudden storm. The rain was falling heavily (*drum fingers on table top*), the wind blew fiercely (*make sound of wind blowing*), streaks of lightening lit up the sky and loud claps of thunder pierced the silence (*clap loudly*). I walked along the country lane (*make walking sound on the floor, whilst seated*), getting wetter and wetter. I heard a rustling in the hedge-row (*rustle paper/plastic bag*), followed by some squeaks (*high-pitched squeaks*), then a rat scurried across the path in front of me (*scurrying motion with fingers on table top*).

In the distance I heard a train rumble by and whistle (*choo-choo several times followed by whoooo-ooo*) and above my head an owl hooted (*noise of owl hooting*).

I was getting very wet and cold, when suddenly ahead of me I saw a large house. I thought I would see if I could shelter there until the storm had passed. I walked up the path to the front door (*make walking sound with feet*) and knocked loudly (*knock on table top*). Inside I heard a dog barking (*make barking noise*). I waited, but no one came, so I knocked again even more loudly (*knock on table top*). Suddenly, the door swung open with a creak (*make creaking sound*). I walked into the large entrance hall and called 'Hello' (*everybody call 'hello'*). There was no reply so I shouted again 'Is anybody there?' (*everybody shout 'Is anybody there?'*). Still no answer, just silence. All I could hear was the rain drumming on the window-panes (*drum fingers on table-top*) and the wind blowing through the dark passage ahead (*make sound of wind blowing*).

A black cat walked down the stairs and miaowed as it passed me (*miaow like a cat*) and once again I heard the barking of a dog (*make barking noise*). It seemed to coming from upstairs. Slowly and quietly I began to walk up the stairs (*make slow and quiet walking sound with feet*). As I approached the first bedroom, I heard a rustling noise (*rustle paper/plastic bag*). I started to push open the creaky door (*make creaking sound*), then I stopped suddenly. Ahead of me I saw a ghostly figure and heard a terrifying noise (*make ghostly wail*). I turned and ran back down the stairs (*make loud running sound with feet*). I raced out of the front door, slamming it shut behind me (*bang hand down on table top*). As I hurried down the path (*make running sound with feet*), I heard someone shouting 'Stop!' I turned to look and there, framed in the open doorway, stood a women smiling at me. 'I'm so sorry', she said 'I was just changing the bedding and I got tangled up in the duvet cover. Can I help you?' I breathed a long sigh of relief (*make long, loud sigh*).

The End (*everybody claps*)

POPULAR DANCE ROUTINE

L2; ! – be aware of any members who
may be unsteady on their feet

Equipment

Choose a popular CD that is currently in the charts. It should have a strong, regular beat that is not too fast.

What to do

1. Play the CD to members. Explain to them that they are going to make up a dance routine to go with the music.

2. If you feel that some of your members are sufficiently capable you could give them the option of either making up their own with a partner, or in a small group whilst the rest follow your routine. Otherwise, work with the whole group together.

3. Practise some dance movements with them such as:

    •   step to the right/left/forwards/backwards

    •   kick to the right/left

    •   roll hands

    •   hitch-hike over right/left shoulder

    •   hands on hips and sway

    •   cross hands over chest and sway

    •   pivot on one foot

- click fingers to right/left of head

- march on the spot

- cross right foot over left in front/behind

- wave arms above head.

4. You can also ask the participants if they know of any other suitable dance moves. Tell the group they will have around twenty minutes to think up and practise a routine. Encourage those that have opted to create their own routine to keep it fairly simple.

5. Play the CD over and over while you teach a routine to your group.

6. After the allotted time, call everyone back together and ask each group/pair to demonstrate what they have learnt.

OUTSIDE EVENTS

Many people with a learning disability have limited resources to pay for club activities and it can therefore be difficult to find suitable outside events that will cater for all your members' budgets.

Transportation can prove the most expensive outlay, so local visits are a more desirable option as the normal transport available can usually be re-routed to the chosen venue.

For a distance that is beyond an acceptable mileage for using a car, coaches or mini-buses will be required, but it *is* good to venture outside familiar areas from time to time. Grants or sponsorship from a local business may help off-set some of the costs, and local groups such as the Lions or Round-Table can be generous with their donations.

Outside events require considerable forward planning. You will need to make sure that your group has the appropriate insurance for taking people outside your usual setting.

It is good practice to make a pre-trip visit in order to write up a risk assessment, which can then be shared with staff and helpers. (Remember that meeting up with, and departing from, the coach can also be a risky business and should be included in your assessment, along with members' medical conditions, behaviour and any other unusual requirements.) When writing a risk assessment, it is a good idea to take a virtual tour of your outing to anticipate possible problems that might occur and consign these to paper under the heading 'Risk'. Next to this, a second heading 'Action' should be used to detail the preventative measures that should be taken. (An example is given in Figure 9.) Keep the wording brief and to the point. As an official document, it will require details such as:

- date
- times – departure and return
- destination
- anticipated numbers (specify number of helpers)
- signatures (writer and approver)
- a section listing individuals with potential problems such as dog phobias.

Number each page and staple together.

You will obviously need additional staff for outside events. Make sure that you give extra helpers plenty of notice and check that everyone involved has a current Criminal Record Disclosure which can take from two weeks to several months. If this is not possible in the time available before the event, invite parents and carers to accompany their own charges. Good volunteers are hard to come by, so ensure that helpers do not have to contribute to the cost of any outings as you do not want to lose their good-will. Try and ensure that you have sufficient funds available to cover their fares.

FROME GATEWAY CLUB

OUTING TO EXMOUTH

Saturday 5th July 2008

Coach departs Badcox car park at 9.00 a.m. and returns 9.00 p.m.

24 members   18 helpers

Risk	Action
Danger from moving cars at coach pick up point.	Assemble waiting group in pedestrian area and escort small groups to coach.
Sickness on funfair ride.	Limit food and drink intake before ride. Discourage nervous members from riding.
Prone to wander off: Mandy Ali Grace.	Epileptic: John Lee.

Figure 9

You will need to divide your club members into small groups of around six – and whenever possible do this prior to the trip. Take into account the mobility and interests of the participants and ensure that each small group has two helpers. Generally speaking, a ratio of one helper to three members is acceptable, but where mobility or behaviour is a particular issue, you may need to provide one-to-one assistance.

Provide each helper with a list of the club members in their group and also, the mobile phone numbers of other helpers in case assistance should be required. Each club member should wear a badge disclosing their first name and the organizer's mobile-phone number in case the member becomes lost or involved in an emergency.

Letters detailing the trip should be sent home well in advance of the outing. The letter should be clear about the times of departure and return, any money that will be required, packed meals and suitable clothing. It should also include details of the destination and activities involved.

Your organization will undoubtedly have its own policy on members' medication. It is probable that some will need to take tablets during a day's outing. If such members are not accompanied by their own carers, you will need to find a helper who is prepared to take on the responsibility of supervising and maybe administering medication. Medication must be clearly labelled with the person's name, contents and time required.

When you are planning a trip, you need to check out toilets, parking areas, wet weather shelter and entertainments available. If you are undertaking a long journey, you will need to include a toilet stop on route. Work out the various time allowances and ensure that everyone knows when and where to catch the bus home. Check everyone by name before setting off, including after a toilet stop.

We have compiled a list of useful items to take on outings that you may find helpful:

- first aid kit
- mobile phone
- sick bags/bucket
- radar key for disabled toilet
- change of clothes (especially underwear)
- kitchen roll
- baby wet wipes
- camera
- whistle

- some money bags
- pen and paper
- rain capes
- torch.

BARBECUE

L3; W/Ch; ! – be aware of any dietary conditions
or health issues relating to activities

Our group is fortunate to be supported by our local Lions Club and one of its members invites us to his farm, where they serve a superb barbecue.

Whilst waiting for the food to cook, the members can enjoy rides around the farm on a land train, play skittles or have a go on a coconut shy.

If you are unable to enjoy a similar opportunity in your area, it is possible to produce your own event.

Venue

If you do not have access to a large garden you could try your local country park or a school in the neighbourhood. Make sure that toilet facilities are available.

Equipment

If you do not have access to barbecue sets, you can now buy disposable trays fairly inexpensively (allow one tray per five diners). Ensure that you have a heatproof surface available. You will also need cooking and serving utensils, matches, paper plates, napkins, a drinks table and a serving table. It is advisable to use tape or chairs to mark off the 'hot' areas. You will need to take buckets and some cold water if none is available nearby. You will also need to take any equipment for activities after eating (see below).

Food

Unless you are an experienced and proficient barbecue chef, keep the menu simple – e.g. two sausages and one burger per person. Kebabs are fun if you are working with a smaller number, and you can make your own from a selection of meat pieces, mushrooms, peppers, cherry tomatoes and onion wedges. Pre-cut the rolls ready for the cooked food and offer tomato sauce, fried onions, relish and salad as accompaniments. You can also offer cakes and fruit as dessert. Squash, water and soft drinks can be dispensed from the drinks table. Be sure to cater for vegetarian and other dietary requirements.

Hygiene

Hygiene is a very important consideration when having a barbecue and great care must be taken to avoid any cross-contamination. Ensure that all the meat is fully defrosted and keep the raw sausages and burgers in cool boxes away from the cooked food. Have a bowl of hand-washing water or wet wipes available nearby. Take care that all meat is thoroughly cooked, by checking the middle of the sausages and burgers.

Safety

Cordon off all areas of risk. Ensure that sharp knives and other potentially dangerous utensils are not left unsupervised. Check safe surfaces for barbecue sets and keep buckets of cold water handy for plunging hands into in case of burns. Encourage careful eating and, in particular, warn of very hot foods.

Activities

It's not desirable to spend the whole session eating, so try and plan some other activities such as:

- make your own kebab

- ice your own small cake

- play rounders
- hire an entertainer
- dance to music
- have a sing-along.

SHORT WALK CONCLUDING IN A PUB VISIT

L3; W/Ch; ! – ensure there are sufficient helpers for wheelchair users and others with mobility problems

People with learning disabilities may view walking as a chore and see taxi or mini-bus as the usual method of getting around. They therefore need the proverbial 'carrot in front of a donkey' incentive to make the idea more attractive! The carrot in this instance is a visit to a local pub.

Ideal venues for the walk itself include country parks, canal towpaths and the grounds of stately homes or other visitor attractions close to a suitable pub. The latter often have walkways with good footing and toilet facilities, but you may need to ask permission to take your group into such a property. You may have to provide transport to a suitable site, unless you are fortunate enough to have good facilities close to your base.

If you are limited to walking in a built-up area, you can add interest and enjoyment by setting a challenge of things to observe and items to collect. For example:

Things to spy

- A church

- A blue car

- A cat

- A yellow flower

- A clock

- A blackbird.

Items to collect (wear surgical gloves)

- A screw

- An empty can

- A leaf
- A feather
- A yellow pebble
- A piece of rubbish.

Alternatively, you could devise a quiz sheet with questions relating to your route e.g.

1. What number is the house with the blue gate
2. What does Marco's shop sell?
3. How far is the village of Knockley on the signpost?
4. What animals do they have in Highground Farm?
5. What hours is Maybury's open on a Wednesday?
6. How many windows can you see from the road in Church Cottage?

For observation and collection walks, remember to provide pencils and collection bags. If walking on roads or in crowded places, high-visibility jackets for helpers would be a safety advantage.

Make sure that your first walk with the group is a short one and well within the participants' capabilities, as blisters first time round will not encourage a second outing! Ensure that members arrive with suitable footwear and clothing, including wet weather protection in case of a shower en route.

Sadly, not all pubs welcome people with learning disabilities and those that do, like to be prepared for a large group by advanced warning to allow for sufficient staff. Visit the pub prior to making any arrangements to assess its suitability. For example check if there is wheelchair access, whether the toilet facilities are adequate, whether there are any pub cats that might affect allergy sufferers, or whether there are likely to be any dogs in the bar that might upset someone with a dog phobia? Although a public building has an obligation to provide disabled access, in practice, narrow corridors and tight corners can make wheelchair access virtually impossible.

Prior to your visit, check if there are any members who should not be drinking alcohol because of their medication. You will need to keep a careful eye on these and any other members who you think may have 'one too many'. For some, a diet option drink may be a consideration.

It is important that people with learning disabilities are allowed freedom of choice as far as is practical and safe. Also, it is good practice for them to order their own drinks, although help should be available where language difficulties hinder communication or understanding of money is poor. Members with mobility problems may also need help with carrying drinks to their tables.

There may well be reluctance to walk further once everyone is settled into a comfortable pub, so it is advisable to schedule this visit for the end of the evening out.

SEASIDE VISIT

> L3; W/Ch; ! – some members may need
> to take medication during the trip

For most people with learning disabilities, who live a considerable distance from the coast, a seaside visit can entail a long day trip and involve considerable detailed planning so a trip organized by someone else will be particularly appreciated.

If you are planning an outing to the coast, you need to choose your destination carefully and consider the mobility problems and the diverse needs and interests of your group. Also, consider the weather – June has more daylight hours to enjoy and may be warmer than September.

Check out staff availability for the day of your planned outing and make sure that it does not clash with any local event normally enjoyed by your group members.

It is advisable to visit the area of your planned trip so you can thoroughly check out the area beforehand. While there, get hold of a street map and assess the following:

- availability of items of interest, e.g. land train, boat trips

- location of toilets *en route* and at your destination

- suitable routes for wheelchair users

- wet-weather shelters

- suitable coach drop-off and pick-up points

- affordable cafes

- suitable meeting places

- special events.

Items of interest

Collect together information about opening, running times and costs involved and find out if places of interest are accessible to all-comers. Special considerations need to be taken at venues such as funfairs, and guidance may need to be given on the day about amounts of money to spend in amusement arcades.

Toilets

It is possible to purchase disability toilet radar keys from local tourist information or council offices. These enable entrance to most public toilets for the disabled, where greater space allows carers to assist wherever necessary. It is helpful to mark the location of the public toilets on your map.

Wheelchair routes

Steep slopes and narrow passages along sea fronts to parks and shops should be assessed for suitability for wheelchair users, prior to the visit, in order to avoid unnecessary distress and difficulties on the day.

Wet-weather shelters

The weather is sometimes at its worst at the seaside, so it is wise to look out for suitable places to shelter during a heavy downpour. A local park may provide a pleasant area to picnic if nothing is available along the sea-front. If possible, spy-out an all-weather attraction in case of inclement weather. Alternatively, a local church may be willing to make their hall available as a shelter, which is a better alternative to returning home prematurely.

Affordable cafés

Check out a few eating places with suitable menus at a reasonable price and ascertain if they are happy to accommodate small parties of adults with learning disabilities. Try to ensure that the whole group does not descend on one café at the same time (unless there has been a prior agreement).

Suitable meeting points

In order to accommodate all the varied interests of your members, your group may need to split up into smaller parties. It is helpful to have a base or meeting point. In some seaside venues, it is possible to hire a beach hut (ask the council or tourist information office). This provides a handy place to store packed lunches, wet weather gear, etc. and to make hot drinks. Groups could take turns to mind it and everyone knows where to return to if they become separated from their group. Failing this, a beach tent can offer the necessary storage space. A flag attached to a bamboo cane provides a useful marker.

Special events

The local Tourist Information Centre should be able to furnish you with the details of any events or attractions occurring at the time of your visit. Whilst this can undoubtedly add 'zing' to the occasion, remember that there can be access problems relating to road closures or heavy traffic.

Co-ordinator's role

The co-ordinator's initial role is to check out all the arrangements and prepare a risk assessment, then send letters with all the relevant details home and ensure that helpers are well briefed.

On the day of the trip, it is advisable for the co-ordinator to remain without a group or individual responsibility in order to be free to oversee the welfare of all the other groups. The role of the co-ordinator is to check people on and off the coach, to monitor everyone's whereabouts and to be available in case of a crisis. The co-ordinator's mobile phone number can be included on each member's name badge in case anyone becomes lost.

Swimming

You need to agree a policy about swimming before the trip and give details in the letter home. Many will want to paddle, so a few spare towels and a change of clothing in case of unplanned dips would be a good idea. Talcum powder is great for dusting sand from between toes.

Hot sun

Advise your members to take sun hats, high-factor sun creams and extra drinks to avoid dehydration. Make sure that cream is properly applied and topped up throughout the day. You may find that a whole day at the seaside is too much for your members. As a club, we have successfully combined it with another attraction at little extra cost. For example, we have visited a donkey sanctuary and a museum prior to spending time on a beach.

SPONSORED WALK IN A LOCAL PARK

> L3; W/Ch

There is a feel-good factor to earning money that can be invaluable to a person with a learning disability. To some, it may come as a novel experience but, once they have grasped the concept, helping to build funds for their club through their own efforts, can be immensely satisfying.

Although a sponsored walk brings benefits to those whose exercise is limited, a potential problem with any outdoor event is that it is at the mercy of the elements. It may be advisable, therefore, to have contingency plans in the event of inclement weather.

A small local park can offer an ideal venue. Even walkways and a secure perimeter provide a safe environment, but you may need to check opening times and ensure that toilet facilities are available. It is important to avoid unnecessary problems by contacting the local council to inform them of your planned activity, seeking permission well in advance of the activity.

Prepare for your fundraising walk before the event by canvassing your members. Inform them that:

- We need money in club to pay for all the events and materials.

- We have to earn all or some of that money.

- Collecting sponsorship is an ideal way to raise money for the club.

- Walking is a healthy way to collect sponsorship.

- Practising walking in suitable footwear would be a helpful preparation for the event.

Where carers are unable or unwilling to be involved, try and link that member with a willing sponsor to give them the incentive and satisfaction of walking for a valuable cause. Moreover, if you are able to offer a prize to the member who raises the most money, this is always a desirable incentive.

Send out sponsorship forms early (see Figure 8). Inform your group of the details of the event and give them an idea of the number of laps you would anticipate them walking. Plan for some additional wheelchairs to be available, for first-aiders to be prepared and for refreshments to be laid on.

Map out small, attainable laps of no more than 500 metres, where possible. If your route is a straight A–B plan, position designated rest areas along the way indicated with marker flags, where the genuinely tired can drop out. These areas should be marshalled with helpers to encourage the faint-hearted or report to base by mobile phone, calling for assistance.

It is a good idea to display a large sign that informs the public of your purpose. It might state, for example, 'GATEWAY CLUB SPONSORED WALK. Your patience and encouragement is appreciated!' In our experience, such a display is very helpful in deterring unwanted interest and attention – in fact, potential trouble-makers have even been known to add to the sponsorship! By the same token, it can be helpful to invite the press or a local dignitary to add weight to the event and publicity for your club.

For safety, ensure that all walkers are in sight or in escorted groups. Where laps are involved, you will need to have a designated lap-counter with a score sheet or board to record each participant's progress.

On completion of the event, give each participant a certificate with their name and the number of laps they have completed. Explain to them that they now need to show the certificate to their sponsors in order to collect in their money and remind them to tick off each sponsor as they pay their due. If possible, provide labelled money bags for your members to take home and give them a clear date the money is due in by.

Make sure that you inform your club of the final tally. Not all walkers will make the effort to collect sponsors, so it is good to reward those who do with a medal or small prize. You can enhance the value of these by giving them out in a special award's ceremony (see the section 'Awards Ceremony' earlier for guidance on how to run such a ceremony).

SKITTLES AND SAUSAGE AND CHIP SUPPER

L3; W/Ch; ! – be aware of dietary needs regarding food and mobility problems for participants

Skittles is an activity that most can enjoy, providing there is safe access to the alley. In some pubs, skittle alleys are confined to narrow spaces, whereas clubs are often able to allow more generous margins to the skittles area.

Local knowledge will be useful in locating a suitable venue – however, the best places are likely to be used for league matches and therefore be very busy. Devoting a little time to inspecting likely premises should help you find the best available option.

If cost is an issue, you could opt for a venue that does not provide catering, thereby enabling you to bring in your own food (check first that this is allowed). However, if the establishment does provide food, they may offer the use of the skittle alley free or at a reduced rate. When discussing menus, do not be afraid of asking exactly what will be provided. Sausages and chips or baked potatoes are usually better value for money than sandwiches or buffets. Ascertain the amount that will be provided per head and ensure that the food will be served at a time that is convenient to you.

If you are self-catering, it is possible to make a prior arrangement with a local fish and chip shop. Portions are often large, so one shared between two adults will be sufficient. Bear in mind that fish is not universally popular, so sausages or pies may be a better option.

Divide your helpers into two groups for the evening. The first group will be involved with the skittles tournament and will need:

- a score board and marker (this may be provided at the venue)

- prizes for the highest scores

- someone to replace the skittles after each turn

- someone to organize the players, ensuring that everyone has a turn.

The second group is required to manage the food and will need:

- paper plates, napkins, plastic cutlery, tomato ketchup, vinegar and salt

- a sharp knife to halve fish or long sausages and serving spoons for the chips

- kitchen paper for mopping up spills

- black bin-bags for rubbish

- hand wipes.

If you are bringing in food, arrange for helpers to collect it at an appointed time in insulated bags. Speed is essential to ensure that the food is served hot, so be set up and ready to serve by the time those bringing the food arrive.

Be mindful of any member for whom weight is an issue or who has special dietary requirements. Detailing the meal in letters home before the event should ensure that there is no disappointment on the night. You could, if necessary provide a few salad bowls as an alternative.

Take care when getting people to and from the alley as it is easy to trip over the sides. For wheelchair users and those members who are unable to bend down low enough, you could provide a chute made from thick cardboard or plastic to roll the ball down.

MYSTERY TOUR

L2; W/Ch; ! – take the usual precautions for travel
sickness and for outdoor visits in general

A mystery trip, by its very nature, has to be a surprise! This, of course, may cause upset to people with disorders on the autistic spectrum, who like to know in advance exactly what they are going to do. However, these members can be given the necessary details by their carers.

A trip such as this requires considerable forward planning. Once the destination and route have been decided a coach must be booked and the members informed of any requirements such as sensible walking shoes, money for a meal, etc. that they will need.

When planning your event be aware of any problems that might arise in certain venues. For example, a visit to a farm could cause anxiety to members who are frightened of animals. This is particularly important for those with dog phobias, where dogs might be roaming loose. Make sure that your trip includes a period of 'get-out-and-walk' for the more active participants.

Some ideas for venues are:

- Visit a lake to watch water sports and wildfowl.

- Visit a local airfield to watch planes take off.

- Visit a canal to watch the canal boats.

- Visit an area of natural beauty or interest and have a drink in the café.

- Kite flying and hang-gliding.

You could also consult your local Tourist Information Office for a list of special events in the area, such as a parade, classic-car drive through, hot-air balloon festival, country dance display, fetes. Be aware in your planning that many public toilets close early nowadays in order to avoid vandalism, and also discuss your route with the coach company to ensure that it is suitable for a large vehicle.

If you can, look out for interesting features along the route to add to the pleasure of the journey.